Dedicated
to Jeffrey and David,
my sons,
and my sons in the faith

The Christian Minister

A Practical Approach to the Preaching Ministry

by
Sam E. Stone

STANDARD PUBLISHING
Cincinnati, Ohio   88580

Textbooks by Standard Publishing:

The Christian Minister
   Sam E. Stone
Introduction to Christian Education
   Eleanor Daniel, John W. Wade, Charles Gresham
Ministering to Youth
   David Roadcup, editor

Commentary on Acts
   J. W. McGarvey
The Equipping Ministry
   Paul Benjamin
Essays on New Testament Christianity
   C. Robert Wetzel, editor
The Fourfold Gospel
   J. W. McGarvey and P. Y. Pendleton
The Jesus Years
   Thomas D. Thurman
How to Understand the Bible
   Knofel Staton
Teach With Success
   Guy P. Leavitt, revised by Eleanor Daniel

Library of Congress Cataloging in Publication Data

Stone, Sam E.
   The Christian Minister

   Bibliography: p. 237
   Includes index.
   1. Pastoral theology.   I. Title.
   BV4011 .S866   253   79-63601
   ISBN 0-87239-348-8

Except where otherwise specified, Scripture quotations are from the *New International Version* of the Bible, © 1978, New York Bible Society International.

Foreword

When I was young and without experience, I needed this book. Now that I am no longer young and have had some experience, I need it still.

Sam Stone has a remarkable ability to attend to those innumerable details that the more careless among us ministers overlook or dismiss as unimportant, only to discover later to our regret that large ministries consist of small details that cannot be ignored.

We answer the call to the ministry with high expectations and elevated ideals. We study to master the Greek language and systematic theology; we dream of addressing hundreds or thousands of avid listeners each week. We devour the biographies of the great men of the pulpit, hoping that we may deserve one day to be numbered among them. We believe we have entered the highest calling of all, and we want to be worthy.

We want to be worthy because, even though this contradicts our firm conviction regarding the priesthood of all believers, there is truth in the oft-heard maxim that a church never rises higher than its minister. Every group needs a leader; in the church that leader is the minister. In fact, in the unsophisticated opinion of the masses, he is the church. We preachers love to scold church members for confusing the building with the church, but few people actually do this. Instead, they identify a person, the parson, with the church. It is "Dr. Jones' church." Only if Dr. Jones is a rare and wonderful man will he be able to disabuse his congregation of this error. Until he can do so, he labors with the awesome responsibility of leading the congregation to the truth about themselves and God.

Several years ago Eli Lilly, of the famous pharmaceutical company in Indianapolis, wrote a history of Christ Church (Episcopal) in that city. He concluded that in all the highs and lows of the church's life, the differences could be attributed not to external forces, but to the quality of ministerial leadership. He discovered that among the eighteen rectors in 119 years, only five had inspired the church to move forward. The fortunes of the church did not depend on building or budgets or the national economy but on the ability of the leader to inspire his people. Not all Christians will remain as faithful to their churches as the old verger of St. Mary's Anglican Church in Oxford who informed a group of tourists, "I've heard every sermon and every lecture given in this 'ere church for the past forty years, and thank God I am a Christian still."

What do Christians want in their leader? To whom will they respond? Sometimes churches don't know how to answer this question. They ask for too little, and they usually get it. Can you imagine what leadership qualities would be exhibited by the man who answered this advertisement for a pastor in the 1908 *Methodist Recorder:*

> Must have a small family, if any, and be able to furnish a horse and come to church unassisted. Must not be afraid to work, have no hobbies, have a good clear head, a warm loving heart—and big feet.

Few congregations would list such demands, I hope.

That last requirement recalls the time when W. L. Watkinson of London, a large man in body and intellect, was scolded by his church officers for neglecting his pastoral duties. He answered by putting his feet on the table, pointing to them and then to his head and saying, "Gentlemen, you can have one or the other end. Take your choice!" I didn't hear which they chose.

The desire of most churches would more likely be summarized as in this excerpt from RELIGION IN LIFE (Winter, 1946-47):

A congregation of people want in their midst a man who can lead them into the reality of worship, who can inspire them with brave, clean and moving preaching, who can teach them the relationship between life and religion, who can counsel them in regard to their personal problems and comfort them in their sorrow, and who can administer the business affairs of the parish with dispatch. Note the verbs involved in this list of qualifications: lead, inspire, teach, counsel, comfort and administer. These are the functions of the ministry.

It is a rather awe-inspiring list of expectations. It is one thing to dream of preaching to a large congregation; it is quite another to be their leader, inspirer, teacher, counselor, comforter and administrator. No one is sufficient for such an undertaking.

Should anyone be surprised, then, that we ministers sometimes complain of our burdens, feeling ourselves buckling under the load? The minister wears many hats, too many to look his best in any one of them. He must be careful, in fact, that in his quick-change acts he does not forget what he really looks like. The identity crisis is real. The minister can become so caught up in his multitudinous routines that he feels himself becoming an accomplished role-player, but a disintegrated person.

Here Sam Stone's advice becomes so pertinent. As a preacher-teacher-dean-writer-editor, he has never lost track of himself as servant of God, husband and father, person. When he counsels a young minister to learn time management, he is not stressing just another tool of the trade; he is teaching a principle of stewardship that will enable him to fulfill both his priorities and his personhood. Here is the strength of this book, in fact. Although the author correctly gives hundreds of practical suggestions for efficiently meeting the expectations of the vocation, they are not disjointed items in a list; they are parts of a coherent whole, all working together to make the minister as well as the ministry. The task is important; more important is the man.

Phillips Brooks wisely defined preaching as "truth through personality." His definition could apply to the whole of the preacher's vocation: he is called to personify God's truth, to be the love of God in action, to express the hope and faith of man in God. "No sir," as Samuel Johnson said, "the ministry is not an easy calling, and I do not envy the man who makes it easy."

Easy it is not, but as a reading of Stone's book will assure
you, it is a high and rewarding walk with God.

Dr. LeRoy Lawson
Mesa, Arizona

Contents

HIS JOB

Introduction

I love the ministry.

It is the greatest work in the world. Nowhere else does one have the opportunity to use his talents in a more influential way for God. This book is designed to help the minister become more effective and successful in his work.

Starting with the Scriptural concepts that must guide the Christian minister, this book portrays the real world of a contemporary preacher. It is not a book of theory. The ideas presented in this book are the result of twenty years' experience in the preaching ministry. They have been tested in both rural and urban settings. I have worked as an assistant minister under two men, and have had seven others work as assistants under my direction. Input from many Bible college and seminary professors and a number of successful preaching ministers has helped to assure balance. Their assistance is gratefully acknowledged.

The Christian Minister is designed to help both the preacher who is just starting out and the one more experienced in pulpit ministry. Having taught young preachers for over sixteen years, I am sympathetic to their problems. Each chapter contains questions to think about, a list of additional resources, and project ideas—all helping to qualify this effort as a textbook for practical ministry and related courses. Sample forms, a current bibliography, and workable suggestions on many aspects of his work make the book a valuable resource for the established minister also. This book is a survey. It introduces all of the major phases of a Christian minister's work. Although written from the perspective of one who has ministered with Christian Churches and Churches of Christ, the principles are valid for those in other religious groups. Each chapter is both practical and personal.

Ard Hoven, well-known minister, broadcaster, and professor, summed up the minister's role in this way: "The ministry of the gospel is not simply a job—it is a way of life in Christ." After completing over fifty years in the ministry, Dr. Hoven explained, "The sheer joy of being able to render a needed service under the leadership of Christ is at the heart of a wholesome ministry." This volume was written to encourage all who seek to serve the Lord in this way.

Several years ago a young minister was preaching in Iowa. He was working part time as the county Civil Defense director as well. A representative from the Civil Defense headquarters offered him a job as the state director at a much larger salary than he was making with the church. He told his family, "I didn't feel that it was the right place for me. If I do a good job as state Civil Defense director, in 300 years who will care? But if I can do a halfway good job as a minister of the gospel, in 300 years a lot of people will care."

My prayers are with every minister who reads this book. Even though I am not able to preach to a church every week now, my heart is still behind the pulpit each Sunday. No more vital task exists. By the preaching of the gospel, God chose to bring salvation to a lost world. As we share in this task, we become His instruments. Faithfulness, not fame, must be our goal. Those in specialized Christian leadership roles can say with Paul, "We do not preach ourselves, but Jesus Christ as Lord, and ourselves as your servants for Jesus' sake" (2 Corinthians 4:5).

Part One

THE ROLE

Section Outline

1. The Minister in the New Testament
   A. The Place
   B. The Picture

2. The Minister Today
   A. What Some Are Saying
   B. What the Church Expects
   C. What He Actually Does
   D. What He Should Do
   E. How to Get There From Here

CHAPTER

1

The Minister
in the New Testament

As you read, think about these questions:
—How do you picture the work of a minister?
—How does the New Testament (particularly Paul's letters to Timothy and Titus) picture the minister's work?
—What Scriptural precedent is there for the professional minister?

God works through men. In Old Testament times, the prophets were His messengers. In the New Testament period, He chose apostles and evangelists to proclaim salvation's story. In the years that followed, preachers have been used to deliver God's Word. The Christian minister's role will continue until the Lord returns.

Through apostolic command, God directed the church to prepare a faithful ministry. "The things you have heard me say . . . entrust to reliable men who will also be qualified to teach others."[1] Some prefer to call these men "evangelists," "pastors," or "preachers," but no designation is any more appropriate than "minister." Our Lord described His work as ministry.[2] Often the word is rendered "service." Service is central in the Christian leader's life. The Christian minister communicates God's love to man both by his words and his life.

Since the New Testament nowhere provides a concise "job description" for the minister, many have become confused about his task. From churches where the priest alone may administer the sacraments, through a myriad of Protestant variations, down to the groups that have no "paid minister," confusion reigns. Every true follower of Christ must want to hear and heed what Scripture says. Both the man behind the pulpit and the person in the pew must study and submit to the idea portrayed in the New Testament.

The Place

The New Testament makes no distinction between clergy and laity. It pictures all Christians as equal before God. No Biblical teaching requires a pope, priest, or preacher to stand between man and God. Instead God's Word pictures the priesthood of all believers—a mutual ministry. This does not mean there should be no specialized, trained workers to lead and guide in the church today, but it does alter their role from some of the popular misconceptions.

One of the Christian minister's tasks is to help make the ministry of every other member of the congregation more effective. He is an equipper. He helps prepare saints (a term used in Scripture to describe all Christians) for "the work of ministry."[3] As churches grow, specialization becomes necessary. Many congregations have developed a multiple ministry. A church may have ministers who concentrate in various areas: preaching, counseling, music, evangelism, Christian education, stewardship development, and youth. Each works with the church members, helping them to become better Christians, to lead others to Christ, to meet their problems, to assist in church management, and to develop their abilities for the Lord's use.

God provided gifts so that all Christians might be properly equipped for their service. The minister is not simply "to do church work," but to equip the church members to do the work. The minister will always have particular jobs to do—evangelizing, teaching, preaching, and shepherding. Through these he fulfills his obligation of training Christians to work. The effective minister both serves and helps prepare others to serve.

Three questions are crucial to every minister:

1. How does the *New Testament* picture your work?
2. What do *you* feel that your work should be?
3. What does *your church* expect of you?

Ideally all three questions will have the same answer.

Scripture must be our norm. But many considerations are not discussed in the New Testament. When one steps beyond Biblical principles to specific day-to-day matters, he needs to feel confident about what to do and how to do it. In consultation with the elders who govern the local church, the minister must plan a course of action in harmony with the New Testament guidelines.

The Picture[4]

In their desire to recapture the faith and practice of the early church, some attempt to exclude or minimize the role of the preacher. "We won't have a preacher—we'll just all be ministers, like in the New Testament church," they say. These people forget that 1 and 2 Timothy and Titus are in the New Testament, too. Those inspired letters from Paul picture the place of the Christian minister, by whatever term you prefer to describe him.

Elton Trueblood was right when he said, "To be truly effective [the Christian enterprise] must erase any difference in kind between the lay and clerical Christian. The way to erase the distinction, which is almost wholly harmful, is not by the exclusion of professionals from the ministry, as anti-clerical movements have tended to do, but rather by the inclusion of all in the ministry."[5]

Early in the first century, the apostles made elders responsible for each local congregation (Acts 11:30; 14:23; 15:2ff; 20:17ff). But distinct from their role, other specialized leaders are also evident. Timothy and Titus—neither one a deacon or an elder—were active in local church leadership.[6] Knowing their responsibilities in the early church can help us understand better the need for such a role today.

Paul uses at least four expressions to describe Timothy's job: He is a minister (1 Timothy 4:6), a man of God (1 Timothy 6:11), a good soldier of Jesus Christ (2 Timothy 2:3), and an evangelist (2 Timothy 4:5). No one could object to the use of "minister" or "evangelist" to describe Timothy. Neither should one hesitate to use these terms in speaking of the man who does similar work today.

The apostle outlines in some detail the type of individual who should fill this position. Timothy is not to have "a spirit of timidity, but a spirit of power, of love and of self-discipline" (2 Timothy 1:7). He is to be willing to suffer hardship (2 Timothy 2:3), must flee youthful lusts (2 Timothy 2:22), and should not quarrel, but "be kind to everyone, able to teach, not resentful" (2 Timothy 2:24).

He is to hold on to the faith and a good conscience (1 Timothy 1:19), and be nourished in the words of the faith and good teaching (1 Timothy 4:6). He is to be an example to believers (1 Timothy 4:12-16). He is to take heed to himself and to his teaching (1 Timothy 4:16). God's messenger must pursue heavenly goals (1 Timothy 6:11). Note God's concern with what a man is—not just what he does.

A professor once told a group of ministerial students that a minister needs "the shepherd's heart, the watchman's eye, and the craftsman's hand." This is a good way to picture the minister's role. The preacher needs these qualities and more if, like Timothy or Titus, he is going to do the work to which God has called him:

1. He will be a *preacher* (2 Timothy 4:2). Both publicly and privately, he must be an evangelist—a herald of the good news. He must lead men to a knowledge of and obedience to God's will for their lives. A church has a right to expect a minister to major in this area. One of the most tragic occurrences in the ministry today is to see preachers get sidetracked and forsake "doing the work of an evangelist." Men must study so that they can share God's Word with the people. (See chapter 15 for a discussion of preaching.)

2. He will be a *pastor* (1 Timothy 2:1; 5:1-3; 2 Timothy 2:24-26). The minister should care about the people. Scripturally, the word "pastor" is used to describe an elder. Literally it means "a shepherd." In Bible times the shepherd provided food, protection, and guidance for his sheep. A minister must also shepherd his flock. He must know and love the people to whom he preaches.

Peter wrote to first-century elders: "Be shepherds of God's flock that is under your care, serving as overseers—not because you must, but because you are willing, as God wants you to be; not greedy for money, but eager to serve; not lording it over those entrusted to you, but being examples to the flock" (1 Peter 5:2, 3).

As a minister shows concern for the new Christian, the backslider, the inactive member, and as he counsels those who are to be married, those who have problems, and those who want to know what the Word teaches, he works as a pastor. Shepherding is a part of the work of a minister. He is not the only pastor of a church, nor is he necessarily elected an elder—but his work does include shepherding.

3. He will be a *teacher* (1 Timothy 4:11, 13; Titus 2:15). He can't fulfill the Great Commission if he does not teach (Matthew 28:18-20). He must teach God's Word not only from the pulpit but in Bible school, prayer meetings, and new members' classes. He must teach privately and publicly; one teaches by his life as well as his words. If he does not have honesty, integrity, and character, it doesn't matter how well he expresses himself. His life will teach something else.

4. He will be an *administrator* (1 Timothy 3:15; 5:21; Titus 1:5). In this highly complex society, the administrative demands on the minister of a growing church can become overwhelming. Since a minister is devoting his full time to the work of the church, he can implement and direct programs the elders have designed for the local congregation. He must be careful not to try to do all of the work himself, but to equip the saints for the work of the ministry.

To include all of these tasks under one title, what word is better than "minister"? It is a Biblical expression (Ephesians 6:21 [KJV] and Colossians 4:7, for example). The Christian minister stands in a noble company. Jesus said, "The Son of Man did not come to be served, but to serve" (Matthew 20:28). Paul said, "For we do not preach ourselves, but Jesus Christ as Lord, and ourselves as your servants [ministers] for Jesus' sake" (2 Corinthians 4:5).

Scripture outlines clearly the minister's attitude toward others also. He is to pray for them (1 Timothy 2:1ff). He is to remind the brethren of Bible truth (1 Timothy 4:6). He must not rebuke an elder, "but exhort him as if he were your father." He should treat the young men as brothers, the older women as mothers, and the younger women as sisters, with all purity (1 Timothy 5:1, 2). He is to grant double honor to the elders who rule well, and should not consider an accusation against an elder without two or three witnesses. Those elders who do sin he is to reprove publicly (1 Timothy 5:17-20).

Following are some of the other directions Paul gave to the young preacher:

1. Fight the good fight (1 Timothy 1:18).
2. Train yourself to be godly (1 Timothy 4:7).
3. Devote yourself to public reading of Scripture, preaching, and teaching (1 Timothy 4:13).
4. Don't neglect your gift (1 Timothy 4:14).
5. Be diligent (1 Timothy 4:15).
6. Provide for your own family (1 Timothy 5:8).
7. Don't lay hands hastily on anyone (1 Timothy 5:22).
8. Warn the rich (1 Timothy 6:17).
9. Guard the teaching that has been committed to your care (1 Timothy 6:20).
10. Don't be ashamed to testify about the Lord (2 Timothy 1:8).
11. Strive to be approved by God (2 Timothy 2:15).
12. Have nothing to do with foolish arguments (2 Timothy 2:23).
13. Continue in the things you have been taught (2 Timothy 3:14).
14. Preach the Word (2 Timothy 4:2).

For those who hold the New Testament Scriptures to be normative for the church today, careful study is essential. Just as one may find the philosophy of ministry in Ephesians 4, he may learn the methodology in the Pastoral Epistles (1 and 2 Timothy and Titus).

The church will always need the type of leadership provided by Timothy and Titus. People need to be taught to study in God's Word, encouraged to walk in God's will, and prepared to work in God's way. Since the need for the Christian minister remains, the job remains. God ordained that His ministers be supported by His people (1 Corinthians 9:1-14). Ample apostolic precedent exists for the "located ministry." Those who serve in this way need never doubt the divine sanction for their efforts.

When James A. Garfield became president, a minister went to him and said, "Mr. President, I wish you would give me a position in the government. I feel that I can do more good as a government worker than I can as a minister."

President Garfield looked him straight in the eye and said, "Young man, I cannot offer you any position in the government that would be superior to the ministry. Go home and continue to be a preacher, for there is no job superior to that."

Supplemental Reading

Alexander Campbell, *The Christian System*. Gospel Advocate, 1956
(pp. 60-67).
W. L. Hayden, *Church Polity*. S. J. Clarke, 1894 (pp. 35-47).

Related Projects

1. List every reference in the Pastoral Epistles that states something specific that an evangelist should do.
2. Study the views of various Bible scholars on "the evangelist."
3. List the articles appearing in major religious journals during the past three years relating to the work of the preaching minister. Analyze the positions being advocated.

---

[1] 2 Timothy 2:2

[2] Matthew 20:28

[3] Ephesians 4:12

[4] Since this section specifically presents the New Testament picture of the minister's work, Scripture references will remain in the text. Otherwise, Scripture references will be footnoted as all other references are.

[5] Trueblood, *The Company of the Committed*, p. 62

[6] R. David Roberts, "The Role of the Minister," *Christian Standard*, November 12, 1978, p. 8

2

The Minister Today

As you read, think about these questions:
—What are some of the erroneous concepts of the ministry today?
—How do these views affect a congregation's expectations of their minister?
—What tasks around the church should (and shouldn't) the minister typically be responsible for?

What Some Are Saying

Many inadequate views of the ministry are being expressed today. The following list includes some of these views, along with a brief critique of each:

1. *The work of an evangelist was only for the first century.* Even if there were no Scriptural precedent for the office of evangelist, his duties would still need attention in the church today. Ample Scriptural justification for the role is available, however: Paul charged Timothy to teach men who could then train others in all of the things Paul had taught him.[1] Subsequent church history adds evidence to the view that the office of evangelist was continued in the church after the death of the apostles.

2. *The minister (evangelist) is to establish a church and*

leave as soon as it gets started. This concept was popular in the frontier days of American Christianity and is still heard in some circles today. It was taught that an evangelist had only a limited role with a given congregation—limited by the scope of the "revival meeting" alone. Does the evangelist actually have a greater role? J. W. McGarvey answered this question in his address on "Church Government":

> It is plainly taught that he did. Here again the example of Timothy serves our chief purpose, for the reason, I think, that we happen to know more about him than any other evangelist. He was left in Ephesus, a church fully supplied with elders . . . and he remained there until Paul . . . sent Tychicus to take his place and requested him to come to Rome (1 Timothy 1:3; 2 Timothy 4:9, 12). His residence there covered at least four years, nearly an average stay for a preacher in our day. He was not there as a pastor, or an elder, but as an evangelist (2 Timothy 4:5).[2]

McGarvey thus refutes the notion that a minister must move on promptly as a church is organized and appoints elders.

Some contend, properly, that Timothy held a unique role as an assistant to the apostle Paul. A number of his specific assignments may have been given him not just in his capacity as an evangelist, but as a helper of the great apostle. The fact remains that he did stay to "do the work of an evangelist" with an established church.

Philip was an evangelist; we first see him in this capacity in Acts 8. The account there concludes with his preaching the gospel in several cities "until he reached Caesarea."[3] When he is next seen some eight to ten years later, he is still in Caesarea![4]

A minister might stay and preach with the same congregation for a number of years; at other times he might move on sooner to help another congregation. If a church has capable elders who have the time and ability to preach and handle the other work, and can get along fine without him, that is commendable. But this situation represents the ideal; it is not feasible for most individual churches. Usually the elders are working at other jobs and are not available at all times, as a minister would be.[5]

3. *The minister must rule his congregation.* Some preachers seem to feel that they are to rule the church like a king. They claim that they are "God's man for the position." They want to direct the program "as God leads them." If you

disagree with their program, then you're disagreeing with God!
That's a little frightening, isn't it?

While none can deny the effectiveness of some strong,
domineering individuals in certain church situations, this is
neither Scripturally nor pragmatically the proper procedure. It
does not fit the picture of the Biblical leader. The church is
never under a one-man rule in the New Testament. The apostles ordained elders (plural) in every church. Peter spoke of the
elders (plural) having the oversight. The manner of their leadership was not to be "lording it over those entrusted to you, but
being examples to the flock."[6]

4. *The minister must do all the work.* This idea is not often
stated so bluntly, but it is frequently the subconscious concept
of some church members. Imagine that the situation facing the
apostles in Acts 6 existed today. Some widows are being ne-
glected. Many churches would expect the minister to go from
house to house checking into the situation. If the charge were
true, he should certainly lead in getting it corrected. This was
not the practice in New Testament days. Each church selected
workers who could handle various details such as this (which
are necessary and important). Those who were to preach and
teach were then freed to concentrate their energies and efforts
on the basic responsibilities God had given them.

One evangelical warned church members: "We are stupid
to think we can hire a professional spiritual exerciser who will
wear out his shoe leather for us running from door to door
winning all the souls to Christ and desperately trying to change
their diapers and feed them bottles." He also warned of the
tragedy that comes when a minister is kept so busy doing
"church work" that he has no time to study. The minister then
has nothing prepared to teach his people when they come
wanting to learn the Word. "Unless we evangelical church
members in America wake up to what we are doing to ourselves today by trying to make a professional clergyman do
what God intended us to do, we'll die on the vine."

Every minister must learn that it is better to get ten men to
work than to do the work of ten men. Perhaps you can do
something quicker yourself, but you'll still be doing it yourself
twenty years from now unless you train someone else to do it.
Besides, you are robbing that person of a chance to do his part.

5. *The minister is simply a clergyman.* This is a popular
concept of the minister's role. In many cases he *is* simply a

clergyman, although the abuse of the office does not eliminate the office or negate its importance.

This notion persists even in Bible-believing circles. The same preacher who would become incensed if you called him "Reverend" will call himself "Brother" with similar meaning. (You can see this attitude in articles sent to the local newspaper or the local church newsletter. Every other man in the church is simply "Mr." but he is "Brother.") Someone said, "We don't call our preachers 'Reverend,' but when you call them 'Brother,' you'd better do it reverently!" You *can* use a Scriptural name in an unscriptural way.

There is no precedent in the New Testament for special titles and privileges for preachers or other church officers. Every church has to appoint people to teach, conduct the worship services, and administer the benevolent and other special programs. In doing this, certain individuals may take on particular titles, perhaps descriptive of their functions in the church: preachers, teachers, stewards, servants, messengers. But according to the New Testament, the church has no special priestly class with special titles and privileges—all Christians are priests before God.[7]

6. *The minister should minimize preaching.* Because some have misrepresented the preacher's role, misapplied Biblical principles, or mismanaged their opportunities, it does not excuse us from doing what the Lord commanded. Preaching the gospel is God's method to save those who believe. "How can they hear without someone preaching to them?"[8] "How beautiful . . . are the feet of those who bring good news."[9] God uses preachers.

Many people today don't agree. Ministers need to get involved, they say. Preaching is relatively unimportant. Ministers need to get among the people and get acquainted with their needs and problems. But while important, this is secondary to the preaching of the word of God, which is the primary task of the Christian minister. Such is the conviction of D. Martyn Lloyd-Jones. Lloyd-Jones also surveyed the New Testament on the subject, and suggests that his premise is confirmed by church history: "What is it that always heralds the dawn of a Reformation or a Revival? It is renewed preaching. Not only a new interest in preaching but a new kind of preaching. A revival of true preaching has always heralded these great movements in the history of the church."[10]

7. *The minister should quit his job, so that everyone will become a minister; then we'll be Scriptural.* Telling a person that he ought to use his talents in the Lord's work doesn't make him do it. Neither does it train him to do it. Patient teaching and nurture is required. While it is true that the modern church must definitely move toward the New Testament concept of involving the entire body in ministry, removing the preacher will not accomplish the goal.

Unfortunately some of the church's most vocal critics miss this point. Rather than working patiently to initiate Scriptural reforms, they often walk away from the church, coating their farewell words with malice.

A college student once announced that he was leaving the institutional church to join a house church. He felt that some of the possibilities available there would be more like the New Testament picture of the church. He spoke cynically of the more traditional forms.

The campus minister to whom he was talking advised him, "Analyze the church to assist, not to attack."

The modern church has its faults. So does the house church and every other modern attempt to rediscover Biblical methods. Faults will always be present where there are people. We do not need to leave the church or the ministry in order to come to a more Biblical stance.

This is not to say that many of the emphases of the "renewal" movement are not valid. They are. Most are Biblical. These emphases must not be stressed at the expense of the preaching of the gospel, however. God has already determined that preaching should be included.

Certainly every Christian is a minister. Certainly every Christian must develop his "gifts." Certainly every Christian should find a place to serve in the local assembly. But there must still be professionals—whether we call them ministers, preachers, or evangelists—to labor in the Word. We need men to work like Timothy, Titus, Philip, and a host of unnamed leaders in the congregations of New Testament times.

One can frequently hear statements such as the seven listed above. It should not surprise us, then, to find many ministers confused and discouraged. Some years ago Richard Niebuhr spoke of the ministry as "the perplexed profession." This is a common difficulty. The average minister might expect his congregation to joyfully participate with him in serving God and others, but the wide variance of views on the ministry often makes this oneness of purpose difficult to achieve. But if he is to function well, the minister must maintain a clear idea of who he is and what he has been called by God to do.

Gerald Kennedy suggests that a sense of purpose is needed—the preacher must consider himself as a messenger of God who will base his message on what God has revealed in His Word. If he does this, he can avoid much of the confusion brought about by some of the erroneous modern concepts of the ministry.[11]

Inadequate views must be resolved before one is able to turn his attention to what the minister *should be* today. Two other questions may be helpful in this process: (1) What does the congregation think that the minister should be doing? and (2) What is he actually doing?

What the Church Expects

There is always more work to do than one can possibly get done. This is a fact of life that we must accept. One has to draw lines and decide what is most important at this time, on this day, during this week. What is most important in our church program this year? It is all a matter of priorities.

When serving as the minister of an urban church, I once took a survey to ascertain what the congregation felt the minister should be doing. I used a questionnaire to invite the congregation to express opinions about the minister's work. One hundred thirty-six people responded. The entire church staff went over each sheet. We tried to learn what areas were more important to the people than we had realized. Perhaps we had been neglecting some things.

Fifty-nine people actually attempted to make a breakdown of how many hours the minister should spend doing different jobs. Their estimates ranged from a high of 104 hours a week to a low of two hours per week! Five people had time averaging more than seventy-five hours a week. I talked to a preacher in a neighboring church at that time. He had kept a record over a six-month period and found that he was averaging about seventy hours a week for the church. In my own case I was averaging about fifty-five to sixty hours of church work (plus teaching at a seminary and taking graduate work).

Thirty-seven of the fifty-nine people said that the minister's highest priority of time should be given to study. On the other hand, two people allotted no time for study, and nine gave five hours or less. The average time allotted for study was ten hours a week. I think that most ministers would be thrilled if they could spend ten hours a week in study. How many preachers average even this much study time each week? If one does not have time to study, what is he going to have to say? Where will he get something to say?

The discussion of the survey with the elders and later in a sermon with the congregation proved profitable. It became easier for the church members to see the necessity of priorities in the preacher's work and their own need to share in the work of ministry. (A sample of the questionnaire is in the Appendix.)

A minister is responsible to God first for his own soul, next for his family. But he is also accountable to the Lord for the people that he serves. He is to put them in mind of the Scripture and nourish them in the good words of faith. Over and over Paul reminds Timothy that he must strive to show himself approved to God.

What He Actually Does

But what *does* the minister actually do? I am able to give one example from personal experience. I'm not proud of it; in fact I see many weaknesses in it. Still, the following list represents what I *actually did* during one week of my ministry in a congregation:

Made phone calls to set appointments for visitation;
Secured leaders for that summer's VBS;
Talked to potential youth sponsors;
Sent letters to Bible school teachers concerning change of room location;
Sent letter to prospective college-career class members;
Composed prospect list for the new class;
Made sermon plans for next two months;
Read and did research for youth group lesson that I was to help teach;
Sent letters for all gifts received at the church;
Sent letters to all who helped in housing a missionary;
Made list of possible children's church workers;
Phoned report of robbery to detective;

Dictated bulletin copy;

Worked out room arrangement ideas for Bible school, the children's church, and youth groups;

Ordered replacements for items stolen during robbery;

Made phone calls concerning youth sponsors' work;

Talked to Bible school superintendent several times concerning class arrangements;

Talked to other space usage committee members concerning plans;

Secured and read background material concerning a particular denominational belief prior to making a call on a person of that group;

Made phone calls and personal contacts to set up the college-age youth group for the following Sunday;

Fulfilled the elders' request to contact treasurer concerning a benevolent gift and sent letter concerning it to the man;

Talked to two Wednesday night teachers concerning their problems;

Compiled and gave to the church office a home Communion list;

Notified adult classes of those who were sick in hospitals or had a death in the family;

Prepared copy for the faith-promise missionary cards and took it to the printer at request of missionary committee;

Contacted people for bids concerning burglary repairs;

Typed or dictated all copy for the church paper;

Sorted all attendance cards and took any follow-up action necessary;

Made a number of trips to the post office, getting stamps, mailing letters, etc.;

Attended an elders' meeting;

Attended a mission committee meeting;

Attended a college group Halloween party;

Attended and preached for two morning services on Sunday;

Attended and taught a youth group session on Sunday;

Attended and preached at an evening service;

Attended and taught a prayer meeting lesson;

Met one hour with each of three assistant ministers;

Conducted a staff meeting with the entire staff;

Prepared sermons and prayer meeting lesson;

Compiled prayer list and arranged for cards to be sent to all on the list;

Made two hospital calls;
Made nine calls on church members;
Made five calls on prospects;
Met with new nursery leader to go over plans;
Went through all mail at church and handled necessary correspondence.

Activities on Sunday:
Unlocked front doors;
Made sure bus got off at proper time;
Turned on lights;
Turned on P.A.;
Put out bulletins;
Counted youth group attendance in evening;
Turned on P.A. for evening service;
Checked to be sure pew ropes were out for both services.

You will see many things that the minister should not do and need not do. I resolved that I *would not do* many of them again when I went to another church. I kept my resolution on most of them!

Instead I drew up a statement of what the minister today should do and be. I shared this list with the elders of the next church I served, and before I went there, they shared it with the deacons and the entire congregation. In the statement (which follows), I spelled out some of my convictions about the work of the minister today.

What He Should Do

A minister must be himself. He must be no play actor. He must not wear the gray-flannel suit of conformity but the camel's-hair garment of honesty. He must seek to learn and teach all that is true. He comes not to fill his predecessor's shoes but to be his own man.

A minister must study. The canned sermon, the opinionated tirade on current events, the warmed-over offering from the proverbial sermon barrel—these are not enough. Men are hungry for the living Word. The minister must be an expositor of Scripture.

A minister must call. It is not enough to lock one's self behind cloistered walls and study. Jesus went also to the marketplace. Paul taught men from house to house. Our Lord pronounced a blessing on those who visit the sick, the imprisoned, and the needy.

A minister must organize. The twentieth century places complex demands on the life of a minister. He will not be able to do everything that he wants to do himself. He must accept the axiom that it is better to get ten men to work than to do the work of ten men. He must inspire and lead others.

A minister must relax. The day off, the "coffee break," the vacation—these are times a minister must have. The man who is always available is not worth much when he is available. If a man is to do his best work, he must be at his best both physically and mentally.

A minister must love his people. If the work of a minister is done only out of a sense of duty or a desire to collect a paycheck, sad will be the results. A minister must be involved with his people. He must rejoice with those who rejoice and weep with those who weep. He should be an example in thoughtfulness.

A minister must seek to grow spiritually. Ironically the press of church work—preparing lessons, sermons, etc.—often robs a minister of his own moments with God. No amount of study or sermon preparation can make up for his own devotional reading of Scripture. No amount of praying with the sick, the bereaved, and various groups can make up for a lack of private prayer.

A minister must work with others. He is not a dictator. He is not a "one-man show." His opinion is not always the right one, nor the best one. He must be willing to serve under the direction of the elders and to share in decision-making with other church leaders.

A minister must be interested in world evangelism. Winning the lost must not be limited to the local area. The church of Christ must reach out or it will pass out; it must evangelize or fossilize. Missionary outreach must never be sacrificed for "the local program."

A minister must learn beyond his congregation. It is the height of egotism to assume that "we" have a corner on the truth. The minister will try to learn better methods of church operation and more accurate understanding of Scripture from all sources. Opportunities arise for meeting with believers from other religious groups. We can learn from, and, in turn, share with those whom we meet in such programs.

A minister must serve beyond his congregation. Even though free churches have no denominational headquarters to assign the minister tasks, it does not mean that he is to avoid work beyond the local congregation. Service in camps, revivals, ministerial groups, conventions, and conferences, enrich his experience and extend the outreach of the local church. These opportunities help the total cause of Christ.

A minister must provide for his family. This provision includes more than keeping a parsonage roof repaired and the traditional "chicken every Sunday" available. A minister must provide love, understanding, and spiritual guidance for his family as well. A minister is responsible to be a good husband to his wife, a good father to his children, a good son to his parents, and a good neighbor in the community. According to Paul, if he does not provide for his own, he is worse than an unbeliever.

A minister must be God's man. This is the single most important requirement. The minister, too, must live in such a way that he saves his own soul. Paul knew the fearful possibility that, after preaching to others, he could still be lost. The minister is not above temptation; he is not above sin; he is not above backsliding. He needs the prayers and support of faithful Christians. He needs the help of the Lord to do the Father's will. His goal should be—"not to be served, but to serve."

How to Get There From Here

The minister provides his real spiritual leadership by his example. While it is good to tell his congregation that they are all ministers of God, he must back up his words by involving all his people in ministry. Unless he does, the congregation will not reach the goals he has set for them. The most important factor in achieving these goals is the example set by the minister himself.

Larry Richards has suggested specific ways in which the minister can help to bring about Scriptural changes within the work of the church. "He can encourage the development of small groups. He can introduce participative elements into the meetings he leads . . . He can help boards, committees, and the church at large to focus on goals. He can encourage the expression of divergent viewpoints, and help these groups learn to handle disagreement, thus moving toward a consensus process. He can set a personal example of openness and honesty that will help all in the congregation come to trust him, even though they may not agree with all his ideas. He can teach the Word of God, and help all the people look into it to discover who they are and what they are to be as the church."[11]

We must recognize that the average church member has only a limited knowledge of what the Bible says about the ministry. Remember that all of us are conditioned by our past experience and personal preferences to expect that the preacher will fit into a certain mold. With patience, love, and understanding, seek to lead the congregation to the Biblical ideal.

When you don't feel it is the best use of your time to do a certain job, take care that you don't give the impression that you feel you are too good to do it. Jesus could have been studying or preaching when He was washing the disciples' feet, but He cared about them enough to show His love through the servant relationship. He was not too big to do the littlest job. And, when you let go of a job, be sure that the job still gets done—if it is worth doing! When the apostles were approached with the job of "waiting tables" in Acts 6, they didn't say, "That's not our job," and promptly forget it. They encouraged the church to find other competent people to do it. So must we. Proper training and motivation are essential at this point.

All of God's work is important—and all of it must be done. As we use our abilities for the Lord, we must help every other Christian develop his. In this way, all can help build up the body of Christ.

Supplemental Readings

Paul Benjamin, The Equipping Ministry. Standard, 1977.
John Henry Jowett, The Preacher: His Life and Work. Harper & Bros., 1912 (Ch. 5).
Gerald Kennedy, The Seven Worlds of the Minister. Harper & Row, 1968.
Wayne E. Oates, The Christian Pastor. Westminster, 1951.
Larry Richards, A Theology of Christian Education. Zondervan, 1976 (pp. 129-164).
James S. Stewart, Heralds of God. Hodder and Stoughton, 1952.
John R. W. Stott, The Preacher's Portrait. Eerdmans, 1961.

Related Projects

1. Secure job descriptions used by three ministers in your area. Write one that is acceptable for you.
2. Prepare a survey that you could use to determine the concept that a local congregation has of the minister's work.
3. If you are involved in a ministry presently, keep a list of all of the work-related jobs that you actually do during one week. Keep track also of the total number of hours spent.
4. Go through the list under "what he actually does" and check the duties that might better have been handled by another. Put an X by the items that should have priority on the preacher's schedule.
5. Write your own statement of "what he should do" that you could share with a church.

----

[1]2 Timothy 2:2
[2]McGarvey, "Church Government," *The Missouri Christian Lectures*, p. 199
[3]Acts 8:40
[4]Acts 21:8
[5]1 Corinthians 9:14; 1 Timothy 5:17, 18
[6]1 Peter 5:1-3
[7]1 Peter 2:5, 9
[8]Romans 10:14
[9]Isaiah 52:7
[10]Lloyd-Jones, *Preaching and Preachers*, pp. 24, 25
[11]Kennedy, *The Seven Worlds of the Minister*, p. 8
[12]Richards, *A New Face for the Church*, p. 226

Part Two

THE MAN

Section Outline

3. His Spiritual Life
   A. Bible Reading
   B. Prayer
   C. Devotional Aids
   D. Spiritual Renewal

4. His Family
   A. Husbands, Love Your
      Wives
   B. Provoke Not Your
      Children to Wrath
   C. Provide for Your Own

5. His Time
   A. Purpose
   B. Priorities
   C. Planning
   D. Procedures

6. His Call
   A. Tests of a Call
      • Ability
      • Opportunity
      • Desire
   B. Other Views
   C. Ordination
   D. Your Call

7. His Changes of Ministry
   A. Your First Church
   B. As You Arrive
   C. Stay Put
   D. Your Contract
   E. To Go or Not to Go?
   F. As You Leave

8. His Study
   A. The Need for Study
   B. Methods of Study
   C. Resources for Study
   D. The Place to Study

9. His Finances
   A. His Income
   B. His Expenses
   C. Good Money Management

3

His Spiritual Life

As you read, think about these questions:
—What is one of the greatest dangers the minister faces in his spiritual life?
—How is this danger manifested in his Bible study and his prayer life?
—How can a minister provide for his own spiritual renewal?

Although he guides the spiritual lives of many others, a minister may tend to neglect his own spiritual life. Bishop Gerald Kennedy has noted this tendency: "A friend of mine who has been in the ministry for many years said what troubled him more than anything else was that so many preachers he knew were really not very religious men."

The truth of the statement should strike terror to the heart of every minister who wants to be a man of God. J. H. Jowett pointed out that the ability to guide others spiritually and one's own spiritual well-being are not necessarily related: "A man may be dealing with 'gold thrice refined,' and yet he himself may be increasingly mingled with the dross of the world. He may lead others into the heavenly way and yet lose the way himself."[1]

The same danger has been described in brilliant satirical verse by Eutychus in *Christianity Today*:

Minister Cheevy
(With profound apologies to
Edwin Arlington Robinson)

Minister Cheevy, man of cloth,
Grew sleek while he assured the matrons.
He feared no wardrobe-eating moth
For he had patrons.

Reverend Cheevy loved the sight
Of crowded pews at Sunday service.
His rhetoric was at its height
When he was nervous.

Pastor Cheevy could obtain
Rapport with tense, neurotic people.
The soothing of his manner sane
Was like a peace pill.

. . . .

Rotarian Cheevy could relax
With all the boys at business lunches.
He knew the art of slapping backs
And pulling punches.

. . . .

Minister Cheevy filled his roles
With balanced poise beyond aspersion.
This guide of souls met all of his goals
—But lacked conversion![2]

The apostle Paul was also cognizant of this danger. He spoke of the necessity of self-discipline and compared himself to an athlete in training for a race or a fight: "I beat my body and make it my slave so that after I have preached to others, I myself will not be disqualified for the prize."[3]

Physical exercise is good, but the exercise of godliness is profitable both for this life and for that which is to come. The minister must determine what his own needs are for self-discipline and spiritual growth. He may be able to do fifty pushups, but he may not be "prayed up." He may have excellent study habits, but need to develop a more consistent prayer life.

The alarming thing about some Christian leaders today is that they seem oblivious to the implications of the message they preach. They can shout about holy living; they can write about the need for devotion; they can teach about Christian behavior—but seemingly they fail to realize that the message must first be obeyed in their own lives.

Such undiscerning individuals remind one of the Boston minister who saw some urchins clustered about a dog of doubtful pedigree. "Well, what are you fellows up to?" he asked.

"Swapping lies," said one. "Whoever tells the biggest one gets the pup."

"Boys! I'm shocked!" the preacher replied. "When I was your age I never thought of telling an untruth!"

"You win!" the kids chorused. "The dog's yours!"

What can prevent the erosion of spiritual commitment? Paul called for self-discipline. He told Timothy, "Train yourself to be godly."[4] One must train and *keep* himself in training just as an athlete does. Elton Trueblood explains, "The athlete who is in training for a contest does not dare relax his discipline for a single day. Thus, Bob Richards, when he was at the height of his power as a pole vaulter, crossed the nation by car. He stopped at a different athletic field every day in order to keep in trim. This is the price of excellence."[5]

Bible Reading

A minister is tempted to read the Bible only for sermons, lessons, addresses, and articles. He reads it to find something to say to someone else. This is not enough. He first must read it to see what God is saying to him. The psalmist declared, "Thy word have I hid in mine heart, that I might not sin against thee."[6] Today many seem content to stop with the first five words: "Thy word have I hid"!

Our Bible lies on the table underneath the television or sports magazine. Like medicine, it doesn't help unless we use it. But when we do, God's Word heals our spiritual ills. Whatever method or schedule of Bible reading we intend to use, we must decide to reserve a specific time from our schedules to read from the Word of God.

Such was the admonition of Jowett in his book, *The Preacher: His Life and Work*. Jowett also noted that often we attempt to measure our success by how fast and how far we are traveling that week: "We are not always doing the most business when we seem to be most busy. We may think we are truly busy when we are really only restless, and a little studied retirement would greatly enrich our returns."[7]

Many varied plans of Bible reading have been suggested. Following are a few that my students have recommended:

1. Reading nine chapters a day takes one through the New Testament every month. This could be done in about thirty minutes each day.

2. Four or five chapters a day will take one through the entire Bible in a year.

3. Variations include dividing the Bible into sections and reading one book from each section consecutively. Other charts provide ideas for reading some from the Old Testament and some from the New Testament each day.

4. Follow a Bible "Book of the Month" plan at church. Let your reading (and that of the congregation) go along with the sermons.

5. A Chinese man who became a Christian had as his motto, "No Bible, no breakfast." He would never eat in the morning until he first had read his Bible.

6. Billy Graham has stated that he attempts to read five Psalms and one chapter of Proverbs every day. He says, "I read Psalms to keep right with God and Proverbs to keep right with man." This takes you through both books every month.

Whatever plan for Bible reading we choose to adopt, we must strictly follow it. That will not be easy. Some years ago, I encouraged every member of my congregation to follow a plan of Bible reading during the calendar year. Many of us took part in the plan. One of those was a professor at a seminary, and he talked to me about his experience. "All through the first part of the year I kept up with my Bible reading every day without missing," he said, rather sheepishly. "But during the summer, I served as an interim minister with a church. I found that I got so busy in my church work that I didn't keep up with my Bible reading." Most of us in the ministry can understand how that might happen. We need time with God's Word.

Prayer

Many a minister has had the following experience: He goes to the hospital to visit a sick member of his congregation, and bows his head to pray for him. Suddenly he realizes that this is his first time to speak aloud with God that day! Such a realization can make a chill go down your back. "Ere you left your room this morning, did you think to pray?"

Prayer must have priority. One preacher made this his goal: "By the grace of God and the strength of His Holy Spirit I desire to lay down the rule not to speak to man until I have spoken to God; not to do anything with my hand until I have been upon my knees; not to read letters or papers until I've read something of the Holy Scriptures."

I find over and over again that when I come into the office and do not stop to pray before starting my work, I always regret it. I find that I don't handle things as well. Problems seem to get worse. And though I may be as busy, I don't accomplish as much. We must set aside daily time with God—as well as arranging periodic hours (and days) of meditation, fasting, and study of the Word.

Prayer lists are valuable. Such a list may be kept in a small notebook. Some like to enter the request and date it; answered prayers are marked through with an 'X' (and sometimes dated). Others keep a general list that they use most of the time, and other pages on which to add specific changing requests.

One cannot help but admire the tremendous intercessory prayers of Lancelot Andrewes. The old Anglican scholar would write his prayer list in great detail and with wonderful scope. What an example this is to show us how many we should be praying for!

Some ministers go through their church membership directory praying each day for specific families by name. This is in addition to the usual intercession for the sick, bereaved, or those having other special needs or problems.

Some find it helpful to pray in the car while driving. (This is one time when it is best not to close your eyes and bow your head!) Others pray when they first wake up, some kneeling immediately by the bed. Most of us want to pray before we go to sleep at night. All of us will pray at meal time. But the admonition to "pray without ceasing" surely calls for something more, a spirit of prayer in life. It is the constant communication with God throughout the day—when one wants to control his temper, when he longs to say a word to help a troubled heart, when he knocks at the door of a prospect, and when he steps behind the pulpit.

D. Martyn Lloyd-Jones offers good advice:

"Above all—and this I regard as most important of all—always respond to every impulse to pray. The impulse to pray may come when you are reading or when you are battling with a text. I would make an absolute law of this—always obey such an impulse . . . so never resist, never postpone it, never push it aside because you're busy. Give yourself to it, yield to it; and you will find not only that you have not been wasting time with respect to the matter with which you were dealing, but that actually it has helped you greatly in that respect. . . . Such a call to prayer must never be regarded as a distraction; always respond to it immediately, and thank God if it happens to you frequently."[8]

Devotional Aids

Bible reading must take priority. We must not spend so much time reading good books that we leave unread the best Book. But other Christian literature, music, and art can be enriching as well.

Every minister should develop a library of Christian classics. If one reads a great book—a classic—it is less likely that he will be wasting his time than if he reads a modern book. These have stood the test of time. One might begin with Augustine's *Confessions;* Bunyan's *Pilgrim's Progress; The Imitation of Christ* by Thomas a'Kempis; Dr. Johnson's *Prayers;* William Law's *A Serious Call to the Devout Life;* and others.

Biographies of great Christians are a constant encouragement. They also provide excellent illustrative material for sermons. The hymnal is also an excellent supplementary source of devotional help. Many helpful modern authors can be found as one becomes acquainted with current literature.

One of the chief faults that I find with television is that it robs me of reading time. Another fault is the lack of control one has over television: I have much more control over what I read than what I watch.

Classical or gospel music can also be inspiring. Music, on radio or tape, can be listened to while driving—making good use out of time that might otherwise be lost.

There are other ways to use the time spent driving for spiritual development. One might secure cassette tapes of Scripture and listen to them while driving. Or one might write out a Bible verse or outline he wishes to memorize and place it on the visor or dashboard. By glancing at it as he goes, he can make time do double duty.

Spiritual Renewal

Plan time for spiritual renewal. Every minister needs such times for himself. A busy man may be tempted to think such times are wasteful and could be better spent serving his congregation in some way. But the time isn't wasted. As Charles Reign Scoville said, "The time isn't lost in lifting a pile driver; and the time isn't lost when a Christian stops to pray."

The familiar words of Ecclesiastes remind us that "for everything there is a season." Many things are essential for a full, useful life. One need not attend church for eight hours a day. On the other hand, does he need to spend an hour every day reading the newspaper or two hours watching television? The important thing is never to be employed by trifles. The priorities in one's life should be ordered; each in its proper place. "Seek ye first the kingdom of God, and his righteousness."[9]

A minister of God must work at being close to God. The church where you preach may have a growing attendance, your salary may be raised annually, and you may be a well-known individual—but God is more concerned about your heart than your outward signs of success. Dr. Garland Bare, a former missionary to Thailand, once said, "God is concerned about what we *are*, not just what we *do*." What an honor when Christ said of Nathanael, "Here is a true Israelite, in whom there is nothing false."[10] The Lord looks at the heart, at one's innermost character and motivations.

It is not enough to teach what is right—one must also live it. Thus Paul commanded Timothy, "Watch your life and doctrine closely."[11] Many live a good life but do not preach the truth. Others are zealous for sound doctrine, but their lives are not consistent with what they say. Both alternatives are wrong. One's lips and his life must speak alike. In this, as in every other way, Jesus is our example.

A man approached a slave about to be sold and asked, "If I buy you and take you to live and work in my home, will you be an honest man?" And the proud slave replied, "Sir, I will be honest whether you buy me or not." This sort of integrity must characterize the man of God. It may be an important task for the preacher to prepare his sermon, but far more important is his preparation of himself.

What happens in this life must always be viewed with the next life in mind. It is this context of eternal life that gives spiritual significance to everything we do. The minister's spiritual life is the most important part of his life. It is one element that cannot be squeezed between two dates on a tombstone. Where you go hereafter depends on what you go after here.

Supplemental Readings

One of the few devotional books designed especially for ministers is Let Us Pray—A Minister's Prayer Book. It was compiled by Paul D. Lowder, published by The Upper Room in Nashville, TN, in 1963.

James H. Blackmore, A Preacher's Temptations. Edwards and Broughton, 1966.

E. M. Bounds, Preacher and Prayer. Zondervan.

Gene Getz, The Measure of a Man. Regal, 1974.

J. H. Jowett, The Preacher—His Life and Work. Harper & Bros., 1912 (especially Ch. 2).

Ralph G. Turnbull, A Minister's Obstacles. Revell, 1964.

Related Projects

1. Keep a record, for one week, of the amount of time that you spend reading the Bible and praying. During the same period of time, keep track of the amount of time you spend watching television and reading newspapers and/or magazines. Summarize your conclusions.
2. Outline a plan which seems workable for you to do better in daily Bible reading.
3. Secure and read one of the devotional classics suggested in the text.

---

[1]Jowett, The Preacher: His Life and Work, p. 42
[2]Copyright 1957 by Christianity Today. Used by permission.
[3]1 Corinthians 9:27
[4]1 Timothy 4:7
[5]Trueblood, The Yoke of Christ, p. 129
[6]Psalm 119:11, King James Version
[7]Jowett, op. cit., p. 63
[8]Lloyd-Jones, Preaching and Preachers, pp. 170, 171
[9]Matthew 6:33, King James Version
[10]John 1:47
[11]1 Timothy 4:16

4

His Family

As you read, think about these questions:
—In what ways might one "love his wife as his own body"?
—How can a minister give the proper amount of attention to his family despite the many demands on his time?
—What family problems are peculiar to the families of ministers?
—What should the minister's attitude be about his wife and children's participation at services and other church functions?

Everything the Bible says about the home applies to the minister and his family. That statement seems so obvious, it should not even need to be said—but I'm convinced that often it is forgotten. He might *know* what the home ought to be like, and be able to tell others how to make theirs right, but his knowledge does not necessarily make the minister's own home all that it ought to be.

Sometimes when we see problems arise in the lives of church members, we think that our families are not susceptible to them. We can explain to others all the rules on how a home should operate, but think that the rules do not apply to us. We must first order our own priorities in the parsonage before we can preach them to the person in the pew. Sometimes we act as if we are better than we know we really are. We must be open and honest in evaluating our role in the home.

U.S. News and World Report featured an article on "Unrest in the Clergy" that discussed the growing problem of ministers who drop out of the ministry: "Pastors often complain of long working hours, low pay and frequent transfers—resulting in unsettled family life and a growing divorce problem."[1]

A man is not marked for life as a disgrace if he leaves the preaching ministry. Some should never have gone into it; some can do more good for the Lord in another profession. But I am concerned when a man leaves the ministry because of problems in the home that might have been prevented, had more attention been given to the principles the Bible gives for all families. The following are some of the basic Biblical guidelines:

Husbands, Love Your Wives

Some specific advice is given by Paul: "Husbands, love your wives, just as Christ loved the church and gave himself up for her to make her holy, cleansing her by the washing with water through the word, and to present her to himself as a radiant church, without stain or wrinkle or any other blemish, but holy and blameless. In this same way, husbands ought to love their wives as their own bodies. He who loves his wife loves himself. After all, no one ever hated his own body, but he feeds and cares for it, just as Christ does the church."[2]

Self love is not improper. You must have self-esteem and self-respect before you can treat others right. The text also calls for Christlike love. This is a love that enables you to give yourself for the other person. Then Paul mentions equivalent love—you must love your wife as much as you love your own body.

Suppose there is one piece of pie left in the refrigerator. My stomach wants it. I love my stomach. It's a part of my body. So I say, "Stomach, get ready. One piece of banana cream pie on the way!" But then I think—my wife, Gwen, likes banana cream pie as much as I do. She's hungry. She'd like to have some. Now if I love her as much as I love my body, I'll go in and say, "Honey, would you like that last piece of pie?" And since she loves me in the same way, she'll say, "Why don't we split it?" That will be better for my stomach anyway!

Or suppose you are very tired. The revival is over. You've been going day and night. Now, finally, you're almost asleep. Then the baby cries. Each of you tries to pretend you're already asleep and don't hear. Your body says, "I can't move another muscle. I need to rest." You love your body; but you also love your wife. She is just as tired. You want that needed rest for her even more than for your own body—so you slip out of bed and go in to check on the baby.

Husbands, love your wives. Consider also Peter's advice: "Husbands, in the same way be considerate as you live with your wives, and treat them with respect as the weaker partner and as heirs with you of the gracious gift of life, so that nothing will hinder your prayers."[3] (Perhaps this explains why some of our prayers don't seem to get past the roof. We don't love our wives as much as we should.)

As a husband, I must respect my wife's feelings. I must consider her interests. My decisions must take into account what would really be best for her. I must resolve that I will not allow "busyness" to be an escape mechanism to dodge my responsibilities to her and my children.

You may have heard of the preacher's widow who had inscribed on his tombstone, "Gone to Another Meeting." David R. Mace understood the danger of neglecting one's marriage relationship, even if it is for a good reason: "One of the great illusions of our time is that love is self-sustaining. It is not. Love must be fed and nurtured, constantly renewed. That demands ingenuity and consideration, but first and foremost, it demands time."[4] The minister must spend time with his wife. Love can die through neglect.

We are living in dangerous times. Crucial problems face every home. Ruth Truman wrote the *Underground Manual for Minister's Wives*. Married over twenty years to a Methodist minister, she was asked about the divorce rate in their denomination. She replied, "According to our church council, a minister can never commit divorce. Murder, maybe—but never divorce!" Surely there is a better alternative than either of those! We can love our wives and make our homes what they ought to be. That works out for everyone's good.

Provoke Not Your Children to Wrath

"And, ye fathers, provoke not your children to wrath: but bring them up in the nurture and admonition of the Lord."[5]

How is this "provoking" done? Some ways are described in the Bible. Jacob showed favoritism. Solomon did it by infidelity and indulgence. Perhaps Eli was so busy at the temple helping other people's children that he couldn't see how his own were growing up. Neglecting your responsibilities *will* provoke your children.

What can prevent this provocation?

Keep appointments with them. The son of a prominent Baptist minister declared, "Every time my dad promised to do something with me, some church member would call and prevent it." Embittered, he returned to the Lord only in his later years.

Watch your expectations of them. Some preachers think they must have a dynasty of sons to succeed them on the throne. My sons know they don't have to be preachers. They don't have to go to Bible college. I will be happy if they do—but only if they *want* to.

Never say to your children, "You can't do this because I'm the preacher and it would look bad." This can never be the basis for a decision. An act is either right or it is wrong. If it is right for an elder's child, it is right for the minister's child. If it is wrong for the minister's child, it is wrong for the elder's child, too. We must decide what is right for a *Christian* to do—not what is right for a P.K. ("preacher's kid") to do.

Be honest with them. You may fool some people who only see you at church—but your wife and children know what you're really like. People need to know that the minister is human, just like everyone else. We need to apologize to our children when we do something wrong. If we're hasty, or angry, or make the wrong decision, the quicker we can admit it the better. Our children are more likely to have the right spirit if they see it in us.

Once when I was speaking in a distant state, a lady said, "You're so cheerful. I'll bet you never get mad!" I told her that was not quite true. I was thankful my wife and boys weren't there to reinforce my statement with a few testimonials!

Our children see us for what we really are. They see us around home without a crowd watching our behavior. Barbara Ryberg's prayer expresses this fact well:

The Greatest Test

Help me to walk so close to Thee
That those who know me best can see

I live as godly as I pray
And Christ is real from day to day.
I see some once a day, or year,
To them I blameless might appear;
'Tis easy to be kind and sweet
To people whom we seldom meet;
But in my home are those who see
Too many times the worst of me.
My hymns of praise were best unsung
If He does not control my tongue.
When I am vexed and sorely tried
And my impatience cannot hide,
May no one stumble over me
Because Thy love they failed to see;
But give me, Lord, a life that sings
And victory over little things.
Give me Thy calm for every fear,
Thy peace for every falling tear;
Make mine, O Lord, through calm and strife
A gracious and unselfish life:
Help me with those who know me best,
For Jesus' sake, to stand the test.

Reserve time for them. My wife is an extra-special person.
Several years ago she gave a note to each of my sons on their
birthdays. The note said something like this: "I want you to
know that any day you want me to spend a half hour with you,
I'll do that. We'll talk about anything that you want to talk
about or do anything that you want to do." They don't ask for
this every day, but they do from time to time.

You'd probably be amazed at what they talk about. My
older boy, Jeff, is a real horse lover—especially Arabians. That's
what he likes to talk to her about. She knows all the parts of a
horse and more about Arabian breeding than I do. Don't you
think that when he has a problem on another subject, he'll feel
free to talk with her about it? He does. She has shown that she
is willing to spend time in what *he* is interested in.

My other son is two years younger. David loves sports. He
likes games. He'll frequently ask his mother to play a game
with him or to look over some sports material. He used to bring
out all of his baseball cards for her to see!

Although both of our boys are teenagers, we have not had
the problem of their "clamming up" and not talking to us. I

don't mean to say that everything is ideal—but I am saying that we have good communication.

We spend our vacations together. A few years ago I was anxious to go to the Holy Land. My wife graciously said that I could go and they would stay here, since we couldn't afford for everybody to do it. But when I got to counting how few years we would have left with both boys, I decided that the Holy Land trip could wait. The boys couldn't.

Provide for Your Own

"If anyone does not provide for his relatives, and especially for his immediate family, he has denied the faith and is worse than an unbeliever."[6]

"Providing for your own" involves more than the obvious original meaning of the term. Your wife needs time and understanding.

Take time to listen to your wife. See how she feels. A Baptist preacher's wife, Mrs. Loren Andis, wrote some new words to the song "Sixteen Tons":

> I was born one morning, heard the church bells ring
> I picked up a hymnal and started to sing:
> Got a preacher for a husband and my-o-me
> Got sixteen jobs plus a family.

When a minister gets home in the afternoon after a long day of talking to people, the last thing he wants to do is listen to somebody else's troubles! But try to see it from her side. She has been home all day and has not had someone to talk to. She has problems, questions, and interests. She needs a "release valve" just as you do. You can provide that.

Schedule time to be with your family. One of the mistakes that I made in the early years of my ministry was trying to do too many things. I felt that they could not have a meeting in the church if I wasn't there. I thought that I had to open the church in the morning and close it at night. I had to be sure everything was going O.K. all through the day. It was all on my shoulders.

As I matured, I realized that this attitude was not right, so when I started my next ministry, I decided that I was never going to start doing some of the things I had been doing at the previous church. If those things didn't get done, they just wouldn't get done—but I wasn't going to worry myself about them. I determined to schedule time to be with my family.

If it means setting a day to be off during the week and going out of town, you should do it. If you have a multiple ministry, this is much easier to do. Each person can have his day off and another staff member can handle all the calls on that day. I found that I had been expecting more of myself than the elders were. They said, "You ought to have a day off, and spend more time with your family." They weren't expecting me to be out calling or at some meeting every night. I was driving myself to meet expectations that were unreal and unwise. God didn't expect me to do it either. God instead expects me to put my family before my job—whatever it is.

During much of my ministry, Gwen and I have tried to eat out together once a week. We don't always make it—but it is an excellent goal.

It's not wrong or sinful to put your family first, after the Lord. In fact, you'll do a *better* job for the Lord if you do this. I know some preachers who will write on their calendar "Friday evening—family." If someone asks, "Are you free Friday evening?" they can say, "No, I have something scheduled." You do not have to say what it is, but you can. It is a completely legitimate part of your life.

After all, your family are also members of the church. You're spending time with church members! They need to know of your love and care and fidelity. They need the security that comes when you demonstrate how important they are because you *make* time for them.

Point them toward God. The greatest contribution I might make to the world is in my child. If I succeed with all others and fail with my own, I've failed. But even if I fail with others, if I can succeed with my own, I'll feel that I've succeeded.

Probably one of my greatest faults as a husband and father is in not arranging better family devotions. I'm ashamed to say this, but I have found it extremely hard to plan for them on a regular basis. I grew up in a home where we prayed at all the meals, but we did not really take additional time for prayer and study together. I have worked to do better on this. I want my family to see that I place priority on the Scripture, prayer, and talking together.

We need to provide guidance, yet allow flexibility. At a

meeting of preachers and their wives, someone asked, "What choice do you give your boys about participating in church activities?" I feel that they have to be in Sunday worship services and Wednesday night Bible study. I think that attendance at these services is basic for all Christians. If the youth group has some social activity, I consider that a "take it or leave it" type of meeting. I would not insist that they have to go to all of these. I do feel they have a responsibility to share in worship, but I would not insist that they attend every single "extracurricular activity" that may come up. I'm glad that my boys want to go to most of these, however.

The same holds true for the preacher and his wife. It's easy to get into a rut feeling we must go to every Sunday-school class meeting, every ladies group meeting, and every committee meeting. This robs time that we can better spend elsewhere. As a minister, I want my wife to be active in a ladies group in the church. I want us to be active in a Bible-school class. I want my wife to do what the wife of any elder or deacon would do. I want to do what any church leader might do. But I don't want the church to feel that they can't have a meeting without the preacher or his wife present.

The question of a wife's role in leadership is a debatable matter. My wife feels that she works best by not being an officer in a ladies group in the church. She is willing to work on any committee or help in any other way, but not to serve as president of the women's guild or as chairperson of a committee. Other wives feel differently. It's not easy to make a hard and fast rule. The important thing must be to build the leadership qualities of the people who are going to remain in that church after you leave. You don't want a program to fall apart if you move to another church.

None of us does as well as he should as a minister, husband, or father. The important thing is that we must want to do better. If we do, we will work to learn how!

Supplemental Reading

For the minister:
Larry Christenson, The Christian Family. Bethany Fellowship, 1970.
Dayton & Engstrom, Strategy for Living. Regal, 1976.
"Marriage and the Ministry," The Wittenburg Door; August, 1974 issue.

For the minister's wife:

Wallace Denton. *The Role of the Minister's Wife*. Westminster, 1962.

Francis Nordland, *The Unprivate Life of a Pastor's Wife*. Moody, 1972.

Kathleen Neill Nyberg, *The Care and Feeding of Ministers*. Abingdon, 1961.

Lora Lee Parrott, *How to Be a Preacher's Wife and Like It*. Zondervan, 1956.

Dorothy H. Pentecost, *The Pastor's Wife and the Church*. Moody, 1964.

Related Projects

1. After reading this chapter, discuss with two other ministers and their wives the question of having close friends within the church. Can the minister and his wife see another couple from his church on a regular basis socially without causing problems? If not, what alternatives are available? How important is it to have a close friend and confidant?
2. *For the married minister.*
   Do one or more of these:
   a. Decide on one thing you can do differently to be a better husband; a better father. Do them.
   b. Ask your wife to suggest a book in this area that she'd like for you to read. Read it.
   c. Buy her one of the suggested books for minister's wives. Discuss it with her afterward.
3. *For the single minister:*
   Consider the advantages and disadvantages of being single in the ministry. Discuss these with an older single minister and an older married minister.

---

[1]"Unrest in the Clergy," *U.S. News and World Report,* November 5, 1974, p. 102

[2]Ephesians 5:25-29

[3]1 Peter 3:7

[4]Mace, *Success in Marriage,* p. 136

[5]Ephesians 6:4, *King James Version*

[6]1 Timothy 5:8

5

His Time

As you read, think about these questions:
—What purpose (or purposes) is the Christian minister trying to accomplish with his time?
—How can the knowledge of his priorities for any specific day save the minister time that day?
—What are some procedural ways a minister's time can be used more efficiently?

Time is irreplaceable. It is the one asset we have that *will* be spent no matter what we do. The way in which we manage our time is a spiritual issue. Christians are to "redeem the time,"[1] making the most of every opportunity. If we use our time well, we establish our faithfulness as servants of God.

In the 1700's there lived an English writer named William Law. He wrote *A Serious Call to the Devout Life*, one of the classics of Christian literature. He included this pointed observation: "He who once knows the value and reaps the advantages of a well-ordered time, will not long be a stranger to the value of anything else that is of real concern to him." Time is the key. The person who can order his time well will become able to keep in order all of the things that are really important to him. The psalmist prayed, "Teach us to number our days aright, that we may gain a heart of wisdom."[2]

Benjamin Franklin declared, "Do not squander time for it is the stuff out of which life is made." Time is an important way in which our very lives are measured. Time-use control is self-control.

In a survey reported in *Church Management—The Clergy Journal*, ministers ranked their personal disorganization as a primary problem. The lack of objectives, cluttered surroundings, and disorganized approach to the work situation all can be included under this heading. Many indicated the difficulty of getting everything done. Perhaps it is best to acknowledge at the outset that it is impossible to get *everything* done.

Purpose

The principles of time-control demand that we first define our purposes. What are we trying to do? Such a survey must include our personal life, our marriage, and our ministry.

Engstrom and MacKenzie consider this especially important for the Christian:

> Management of time thus becomes, for the Christian, management of His time. . . . When times get out of joint . . . when tasks pile up . . . and when things go wrong . . . how often do we stop to ask God if we're doing what He wants us to do. It is His time we're managing, isn't this where we should begin?[3]

Where are you going? Too many are like the pilot over the North Atlantic who was asked by a crew member, "Just where are we?" "I don't know," replied the pilot, "but we're making awfully good time!"

All too frequently this describes our modern frenzied pace. Unless objectives have been defined and goals have been set, we are likely to spend far too much of our time in meaningless activity.

If we take care to define our goals in our work, then we become able to compare our goals with those of the organization we serve. This opportunity is filled with meaning for the Christian minister.

How would you sum up the objectives of the New Testament church? Perhaps Jesus' commission to His disciples is as good a place as any to begin. The basic call of Christ is to evangelize and edify. We are to preach the gospel, baptize those who believe, and train them through a discipleship process.[4] With this in mind, how much of the minister's work is related to the goal of the church? Are we spending so much time on "fringe" concerns that we are forgetting the basic thrust?

Have we become so burdened by the multitude of activities that are expected of us by others (or that we think they expect us to do) that we have forgotten what our mission is? Charlie Shedd recognized this problem: "Our Heavenly Father never gives us too much to do. Men will. We assign ourselves an overload, but never the Lord. He knows what He wants from each of us, and there is plenty of time in His day for things essential to His plan. We do Him a grave injustice when we fall into the habit of compulsive overwork. We sin when we pressure out His wishes for assignments that have not been filtered through divine judgment."[5]

Priorities

The next essential in time management involves priorities. The Christian's choice is not good from evil, but the best of the good. Likewise the minister's choice is not, "Shall I do something bad or something good?" Instead he asks, "Which of the many good things is most important for me to do today?" Priorities are essential.

A minister could spend eight hours a day studying—or calling, or counseling, or teaching, or writing, or preaching. If he did give eight hours a day to any one of these, the other elements of his work would suffer. It is impossible to do everything we should do, but this does not excuse us from doing some things. Of crucial importance is our selection—doing the right things.

The Pareto principle states that the *significant items in a given group normally constitute a relatively small portion of the total items in the group.* In other words, you may spend eighty percent of your time on trivial matters that produce only twenty percent of the results. On the other hand, if you concentrate even twenty percent of your time on the "vital few" situations or problems, this will produce eighty percent of the results. The lesson is obvious. Use your time on the most important matters.

Ministers and other administrators tend to confuse the *urgent* with the *important.* Former President Eisenhower indicated that he discovered that the two categories rarely go together. He found that the really important matters were seldom urgent—while the most urgent matters were seldom important. This points to the cause of much failure in our work. We are so busy with the things that "just have to be done right away" that we fail to do the far more important things that we think can wait.

The account of Charles M. Schwab's challenge to management consultant Ivy Lee bears repeating. Schwab demanded, "Show me a way to get more things done. If it works, I'll pay anything within reason."

Lee handed him a paper. "Write down the things you have to do tomorrow," was the instruction. "Then number those items in the order of their real importance. Tomorrow morning, start working first of all on number one. Stay with it until it is completed. Then take number two and don't go any further until it is completed. Then proceed to number three, and so on. If you don't complete everything on your schedule, don't worry. You will at least have taken care of the most important things without getting distracted by less crucial items."

In a few weeks Charles Schwab sent Lee a check for $25,000.00. The idea was worth it!

Planning

An axiom of efficiency experts is, "Work smarter, not harder." Efficiency calls for planning. The more time spent in planning, the less time will be required for the actual work.

After projecting our goals, we must plot a course that will enable us to reach them. We have only so much time—and it never seems to be enough.

Have you ever stopped to analyze where your time goes? I commend the keeping of a time log for at least a week (preferably a month) to help you find out. It is most revealing—and frightening—and humbling—and (sometimes) encouraging! I once kept such a log for a full month. I found that I was averaging around fifty-five hours per week of "church work" plus teaching a college class and taking graduate study. This helped me to feel better about the things I was not getting done. I was getting some things done—and I tried to do them well.

Once you know where your time is going, you may then proceed to budget for future expenditures, just as you would with your finances. Planning involves long-range programs. It moves from the year in advance, to the month ahead, the coming week, and finally the next day. Every minister ought to be *actively* involved in each type of planning.

A calendar is a must. Experts suggest that a single calendar be kept at your desk. All dates—family, church, personal, speaking engagements—are then entered in the single calendar. This calendar may serve to protect the minister when he is away from his office and is asked to speak at some meeting. He may take down the information, indicate that he will check his calendar, and let the individual know promptly concerning his availability. This removes the pressure of having a person standing over him as he checks the calendar to see if he has something written on the day in question. He might just need the day in question as a "day of rest" and want to keep it for that!

I find it helpful to go through the calendar at least once each day—looking at the month ahead. At least once a week, I glance ahead to future months. This reminds me of needs for planning, study, correspondence, and other matters related to upcoming events. I have learned that the farther ahead I begin working and planning on something, the easier it becomes. I've never started planning too early for an event (whether a speaking engagement or a vacation trip), but many times I've started planning too late.

Every weekend, I plot out my day-to-day schedule for the week ahead. This provides time to take into consideration family plans, appointments already made, study that must be done, and work that may arrive unexpectedly. I like to use individual plan sheets for each day (see sample in Appendix). The sheet is printed on an 8½" by 11" sheet of paper. It includes room for family plans and things to be done at work. "Out" means errands to be run elsewhere. Space is left for matters to be cared for at home. Lists are also provided of people to see, phone calls to make, and letters to write. The column at the left may be used to indicate priorities, or the order in which the various activities would be handled. The sheet may be carried in a Bible or notebook, and it can be folded and carried in one's coat pocket. One might also keep a record of business mileage and calls on such a sheet.

Setting deadlines for oneself is a part of the secret to successful planning. I am writing this chapter of the book over six months before the time that I plan to have the first draft of my entire manuscript completed. If my other chapters are completed on time, and if I meet my intermediate deadlines, I should have no difficulty in handing the manuscript to the publisher at the proper time. If I fail to do it, it will be because I have not managed my time well enough.

Even though I don't get everything done that I write on my list, I know what I have and haven't done at the close of the day. I am more likely to get the essential items cared for in this way. Important things that were not covered can be added to a future day's list. Some jobs I might assign to others. Some I may drop, deciding they didn't have to be done at all! A list gives a strong sense of purpose and direction to the day's work. As the Roman philosopher Seneca advised, "When a man does not know what harbor he is heading for, no wind is the right one."

Procedures

When one begins planning to accomplish his goals, he must work out procedures. Here are ten suggestions:

1. *Be specific in your plans.* Include both long-range and intermediate goals. It's not enough to say, "I'm going to read the Bible more," or even "I'm going to read completely through the Bible this year." You need some checkpoints along the way. *How much* of the Bible will you read this month? this week? tomorrow? Psychologically, there is a sense of accomplishment if you can say, "I've made it this far!"

The amount of time you spend planning for the future can be an indication of how successfully you are handling your work: "The higher up the executive ladder one goes, the smaller is the portion of his time which should be spent on present problems and the greater is the portion which ought to be spent on future considerations."[6]

2. *Delegate work wherever possible.* The person being given the job must understand that responsibility for the job goes along with his authority to perform it. If something goes wrong, don't take the job back. Help to determine what the problem is and how it can be solved.

Reading is time consuming and can be easily delegated. Ask others to read a recent book and let you know their evaluation of it. The reading will benefit them besides helping you. Encourage your church members to clip articles from newspapers and magazines for use as illustrative material for your messages. Many prominent public speakers have individuals hired on a full-time basis to do this. You can probably find volunteers in the church who would be happy to assist you in this way.

3. *Use your telephone to your best advantage.* Have calls screened, if possible. Many matters can be handled by a secretary. Have the secretary ask if you might return the call later. Group outgoing calls together. Use the phone to save trips, set appointments, confirm meetings, and gather information.

Some ministers have found a telephone-answering device to be extremely useful. One can be placed on either the parsonage or the church phone (or both). The recorded message can be something like this: "I'm sorry that I am not available to receive your call at this time. If you will leave your name and number, I will return your call at the first opportunity. Thank you." You can use the device if you are not in the office or if you are busy at the time and do not wish to be interrupted. Most such answering units allow one to listen to what is being said by the person calling. If it is an emergency, the minister can come on to the phone at that point. An answering device will be generally accepted well by church members, providing the minister is prompt in returning the calls. He ought to be prompt with all telephone calls anyway!

4. *Do not go through your mail until more important items have been handled.* When you do, dictate or write an immediate reply to each letter. Only those that require checking for additional information should be held for a future time. Keep copies of all correspondence.

5. *Simplify your correspondence procedures as much as possible.* Use form letters wherever possible. Visitor, new member, and other routine letters can then be handled by a secretary or by volunteer workers without direct contact by the minister. Such routine letters should be signed by the minister, who can, if he wishes, add a personal note at the bottom.

You can also make good use of postcards and note sheets. Many matters do not require a full business letter. The late P. H. Welshimer was a prolific user of postcards. In his more than fifty-year ministry at First Christian Church at Canton, Ohio, he helped it become the largest Christian Church congregation at the time. Despite his busy schedule, he constantly would make use of postcards to pen a few lines complimenting a brother preacher for an article, message, or program. Such a note can then be addressed by the secretary (or the preacher) and mailed. Some ministers write a quick reply at the bottom of the original letter, make a copy of it, and return the original to the sender. Others use "fast forms" that have carbons attached and allow both sender and receiver to keep a copy.

One of the best investments a minister can make is a portable cassette tape recorder. Adapters can be purchased that permit use of the recorder in the car. One might not only listen to sermons, Scripture, or music while he drives, but he might give dictation also. He might stop to call on a family, find they weren't home, and dictate a note that his secretary could send them later. He might record ideas for a sermon or article while they are fresh in his mind.

Dictation equipment does not have to be expensive. Secretaries who cannot take shorthand can quickly learn to transcribe from tape units. The standard cassette-size tape is advantageous because it is almost universally available. A minister might be away conducting a revival, use a tape recorder there, and mail back correspondence and other work that his secretary could transcribe in his absence.

6. *Set limits on appointments.* When someone is coming for a visit, attempt to arrange a time limitation when the appointment is made: "Why don't we plan for half an hour? How would 1:00 to 1:30 be?" Then instruct your secretary to come to the door or call you on the intercom at about 1:25, saying, "I wanted to remind you that you need to talk with Mr. Jones in a few minutes" or "Your next appointment is here."

You can respond, "Thank you. We'll be through here in a few minutes." This gives you a polite way in which to end the meeting. It reminds the other person to conclude, yet does not put you in the position of breaking off the visit arbitrarily. If there is much more that needs to be discussed, a future appointment can be set up.

7. *Plan at night what you will wear the next day.* Have your clothing laid out and ready. It saves time in the morning—and lets you decide while you are fully awake!

8. *Schedule office hours.* Come to the office early. Get a jump on the others and have everything ready when associates arrive. Your "office hours" are the times each day or each week when you would normally be available to receive telephone calls and/or visitors. These would naturally have to be flexible.

9. *Pace yourself.* Many jobs cannot be completed in one day, especially those which might be better handled with some time in between various segments of the procedure. Such time off allows for thinking and reflecting, and your subconscious might help you along on the project even when you're not actively thinking about it. You will be more likely to pick out mistakes if your written material has had a day or two to "cool" since it was written.

10. *Plan only eighty percent of your day.* Some managers recommend that executives anticipate possible crises by leaving twenty percent of their time unplanned to provide a cushion for the unexpected. Contingency planning lets us respond to the real emergencies of life. Jesus taught us that we must not be too busy to help those who need our help.

This advice is given for other reasons, too. You need free time. You need a break. Some time should be allowed in the middle of any work period to relax, move around, and do something less demanding. Students are advised to have such "bumper periods" amidst their long hours of study. Some time for rest should always be set aside: "There is no music in a rest but there's the making of music in it. And people are always missing that part of the life melody."[7]

Supplemental Readings

Engstrom and MacKenzie, *Managing Your Time.* Zondervan, 1972.
Alan Lakein, *How to Get Control of Your Time and Your Life.* Wyden, 1973.
R. Alec MacKenzie, *The Time Trap.* AMACOM, 1972.
Joseph E. McCabe, *How to Find Time for Better Preaching and Better Pastoring.* Westminster, 1973.

Related Projects

1. Keep a log of how you spend your time for one week. Try to include (separately) all of the specific jobs you do.
2. Develop a daily plan sheet that is suitable for your needs. A sample is included in the Appendix.
3. Discuss schedule priorities with your family, your secretary, and your elders.

---

[1]Ephesians 5:15, 16, *5King James Version*

[2]Psalm 90:12
[3]Engstrom and MacKenzie, *Managing Your Time*, p. 24
[4]Matthew 28:18-20
[5]Shedd, *Time for All Things*, p. 65
[6]Engstrom and MacKenzie, *op. cit.*, p. 50
[7]*Ibid.*, p. 27

6

His Call

As you read, think about these questions:
—What constitutes a "call"?
—What are some reasons for the practice of ordination, the ceremonial act of setting someone apart for service?
—By what criteria can a person be sure he has been "called" to the ministry?

When a "call" to the ministry is mentioned, questions often arise. Everyone is "called" to be a servant of the Lord, some would argue. It is true that, in one sense, every Christian is "called."[1] We are called to salvation and service through the gospel of Jesus Christ.

Aren't all Christians called to witness and evangelize? This is true, too. But in New Testament days, some Christians were "evangelists, pastors, and teachers."[2] How did they come to be placed in these positions with these duties?

In other words, how does one get to be a preacher? What needs to happen to him? What does he need to feel, see, think, hear, or experience? Does he need a "call"? If so, what does it include?

Three components are involved in a "call" to the ministry: ability, opportunity, and desire.

Tests of a Call

Ability

The Scripture just cited is preceded by the assurance that God "gave gifts to men."[3] It specifically states that His gifts were given that some should be apostles, some prophets, some evangelists, some pastors and teachers. God endows each individual with evident natural abilities. These talents or "gifts," are given arbitrarily by our sovereign God. When a Christian dedicates and develops his gifts, they will be blessed and used by the Lord. One would do well to ask himself, "What abilities has God given me? How may I best use them for His service?"

Several passages of Scripture help in this study. Romans 12:6-8 reminds us that our gifts differ. Whatever the gift may be, we are to do our best with it. First Peter 4:10 states, "Each one should use whatever spiritual gift he has received to serve others, faithfully administering God's grace in its various forms." All of our capacities are to be developed. Consideration of one's natural abilities goes into determining if he is called to preach.

Timothy received certain "gifts" but, in his case, this evidently involved the impartation of miraculous powers by the laying on of hands.[4] Such powers were limited to the apostles and those on whom they laid their hands.

Opportunity

Chances to speak, teach, and preach might also help a person determine whether God could use him as a preaching minister. Some have come into the Christian ministry from other vocations, after they continued to have increasing opportunities to speak on behalf of Christ. Others who were particularly gifted in teaching and administration have come in a similar way to positions in churches, colleges, and other institutions.

The judgment of the body becomes important. How does the church view your abilities, your character, and your life? Do they encourage you in pursuit of the Christian ministry? We tend to overlook the implications of Romans 10:15—"How can men preach unless they are *sent*?"

Barton W. Stone, a nineteenth-century preacher and editor, was insistent about receiving prior approval before preaching,

and saw support for this idea in 2 Corinthians 3:1 and Acts
13:1, 4. Eugene Johnson points out, "To Stone, there was no
mysterious call apart from the approval and recommendation
of at least one congregation. A man's awareness of God's hand
upon him was his call, which was fulfilled and completed at
his ordination, being the confirmation of this call."[5]

Churches ought to be recruiting their finest young men for
the gospel ministry. Those with ability should be encouraged
to develop their skills through training in Bible college. They
should be provided frequent opportunities for instruction and
service within the local church as well. The church likewise
has the responsibility to send out with its approval only those
who are "duly and Scripturally qualified."

Desire

Do you see the need for preachers of the gospel? Have you
ever looked at the world as Jesus looked at it? He could see the
throng of people and say, "The harvest is plentiful but the
workers are few. Ask the Lord of the harvest, therefore, to send
out workers into his harvest field."[6] He could look at the city
that continually rejected him and say, with tears in His eyes,
"O Jerusalem, Jerusalem, you who kill the prophets and stone
those sent to you, how often I have longed to gather your children together, as a hen gathers her chicks under her wings, but
you were not willing!"[7]

Do His words mean anything to you? Your sensitivity and
responsiveness to the needy world is essential if you are to
consider yourself "called" to preach. Do you have an inner
compulsion to preach? Can you say with Paul, "Woe is me if I
preach not the gospel"?

Seeing the need and desiring to help meet it goes a long
way. Determination can make up for much that one may lack in
native ability. The faithful, dependable laborer frequently is
able to overcome major handicaps when motivated by the tremendous challenge of Christian service.

The three facets that have been discussed suggest what the
"call" ought to include—ability, opportunity, and desire. T. P.
Haley described the aspects of a call to the ministry in similar
fashion: "The desire to preach without the ability is not the
call; the desire and ability without the opportunity is not the
call; but ability, desire and opportunity may be taken as the
divine call."[8]

Other Views

Some have the concept, however, that they must receive a miraculous call. They await a voice in the night, a "sign," or some dramatic incident to tell them that they should preach. No Scriptural warrant is given for such a desire. We have no evidence that Timothy or Titus had some miraculous "call" to their work. They loved the Lord. They had been taught His Word. They wanted to serve Him. They had the ability, the opportunity, and felt that desire—so they became evangelists.

The apostle Paul did have a miraculous experience on the road to Damascus. This was a unique event, however, preparing for his conversion. He was not simply a minister, but an apostle. He was inspired by God to write much of the New Testament. His was a divine revelation direct from God for a specific purpose.[9] Aside from Paul's conversion, there is no Scriptural instance in which any person received a miraculous call from God to the public ministry of the church.

Some say, "Don't be a preacher if you can do anything else." This advice can be misleading. Often a minister has talents that enable him to do more than one kind of work. Certainly God allows each person the flexibility to choose the field of service that he prefers. One might be an insurance salesman, a real estate agent, or a preacher. He could well have talents for all three. The person must ask himself, "Where can I do the most good? Where can I best use my talents? Where can I be the happiest? Where do I have opportunities? What would God have me do?"

He might be a real estate agent or insurance salesman and serve as an active deacon or elder in the local church. In fact, when we first see Stephen and Philip, they are employed in such service with the Jerusalem church.[10] Later, Stephen used his miraculous gifts to do "great wonders and signs." Eventually he preached a magnificent sermon before the Sanhedrin.[11] Philip later is seen as a preacher of the gospel.[12] Many a good preacher has begun as an elder or deacon in the local church!

Ordination

The ordination service does not impart any special powers to a minister. No apostolic succession exists—therefore nothing special is to be expected when the elders lay hands upon someone to set him apart for the work of ministry. However, several important reasons can be given to commend the practice of ordination:

1. *It is Scriptural.* When men were set apart to do a specific work, we find throughout the book of Acts that they were ordained with prayers and the laying on of hands.[13] Sometimes the ordination was accompanied by fasting. In Bible times, this ceremony was used to set apart a person in a solemn service for some particular duty—not always a "ministry," as we think of it today.

2. *It calls for the approval of the elders of the local church.* Each person who preaches should be answerable to his elders. The eldership should not set apart a man unless they are confident that he is morally and spiritually prepared to serve.

3. *It is a practical necessity.* Legal restrictions hamper the unordained minister from performing marriages in many states. The government allows tax benefits to those who are ordained ministers.

In Acts 16 we find that when individuals were "well reported of by the brethren," and had proved themselves by their work for the Lord, they were ordained.[14] Recognition was thereby given to the candidate. The apostle Paul evidently served for some fourteen years before he was "separated" to do his work through ordination.

Your Call

There is no Biblical justification for the idea that one is "called" to a particular church or specific mission field. Such direction is a part of the providential guidance of God. The Biblical sense of a "call" refers to a person's hearing the invitation of Jesus and responding to it,[15] but does not indicate divine direction for every particular decision.

When a person considers his call, he should be neither extremely rationalistic nor extremely emotional. While it is true that he need not hear a mysterious voice in the dark, be saved from certain death, or have a dramatic vision in order to be called by God, neither is the decision to preach a cold, heartless, rationalistic choice. One's experiences and feelings should help confirm a conviction born of careful thought.

God has called men in different ways. Isaiah saw a vision. Andrew and John were called through a preacher. Philip and

Stephen were selected by the church to be deacons, and later became preachers.

So it is today. Some will want to be gospel preachers from their youth; others will decide after some dramatic life-changing experience; others will be dissatisfied with the way they have been going and long for something better; others will be attracted to the ministry for various other reasons.

Rather than feeling that a young person must commit his life to preach, it might be wiser to ask that he commit his life to train in a Bible college and seminary and then use his abilities in whatever avenues the Lord may open up. He might be a medical missionary; he might be a Christian musician; he could be the editor of a national magazine; he might be the administrator of a benevolent home; he might be any of a score of other things. Or he might be a preacher.

Each man should be what *he* is convinced God would have him be. When he is, he need have no fears about his "call" to the ministry. He can say with Charles Wesley:

> To serve the present age,
> My calling to fulfill;
> O may it all my pow'rs engage,
> To do my Master's will!

Supplemental Readings

H. Eugene Johnson, *Duly and Scripturally Qualified*. Standard, 1975. (An interesting survey of "The Call and Its Confirmation")

Related Projects

1. Collect sample ordination service programs. Study the suggested program in *The Christian Minister's Manual*. If you have not yet been ordained, plan a possible service.
2. Discuss with two other ministers how they determined that they should be preachers of the gospel.

---

[1] 1 Corinthians 1:26; 1 Thessalonians 4:7; 2 Timothy 1:9; Hebrews 3:1
[2] Ephesians 4:11
[3] Ephesians 4:8
[4] See 1 Timothy 4:14 and 2 Timothy 1:6
[5] Johnson, *Duly and Scripturally Qualified*, pp. 76, 77
[6] Matthew 9:37, 38
[7] Luke 13:34

[8]Haley, "Our Ministry," *New Christian Quarterly,* October, 1893, p. 428
[9]See Galatians 1:11-17
[10]Acts 6:5
[11]Acts 7
[12]Acts 8:8, 12
[13]For example, Acts 6:6; 13:3
[14]Acts 16:4, *King James Version*
[15]See Romans 8:28; 1 Corinthians 1:24ff; Ephesians 4:1-4

His Changes
of Ministry

As you read, think about these questions:
—How might a college student begin serving in a preaching ministry?
—What are the advantages of a longer ministry?
—What items should be negotiated as part of the minister's contract
  with a local church?
—How should a minister handle an offer to serve a church other than
  the one he is presently serving?

Your First Church

A special thrill comes to a preacher when he is called to
serve his first church. A unique relationship exists between
them, one that time and distance cannot break. Blessed is the
young minister who finds a loving, understanding congregation with which to work in his first ministry!

Many young men choose to begin serving with a congregation while attending Bible college. Some of these schools are
near small churches that cannot afford full-time ministers, but
can pay enough for students to come and work with them on
weekends. Such an arrangement can be advantageous to all
concerned. The goal of the arrangement should be to
strengthen the church so that they might be able to afford the
full-time service of an evangelist who could both preach and

help develop the abilities of all of the other members.

When a person begins preaching, he cannot expect all of the contractual considerations that might be his after he has served in the ministry for years. He would be unwise, for example, to insist on a one-month vacation with pay, four weeks off for revivals, and a book allowance at his first church! Instead he should understand that the congregation is taking him much as an intern at a hospital. The new minister is getting a chance to practice what he has learned in the classroom. The church is not getting the best possible person, but one whom they feel has promise and with whom they are willing to work. Others who enter the ministry later in life, with a good background in Christian service, above average Bible knowledge, and more maturity and experience, may find other alternatives available. Even then, however, most will start in a similar fashion.

A minister might begin in his earlier years by working as an assistant with an older, more experienced person. Just as Timothy served with Paul, and Mark worked with Barnabas, young ministers today would do well to work with a *capable* and *effective* senior minister. Some things can be learned only by experience. The program of a large church is best understood by working with it on the inside. I had the opportunity to serve under two capable men. I learned much from both of them. I learned some things that I wanted to do just as they did—and others that I would do differently. But all that I learned in those years as an assistant minister helped me.

As You Arrive

A popular quotation goes, "You never get a second chance to make a first impression." The way you begin your ministry will affect all that follows. Start with a good spirit, an open mind, and a loving smile for *every* person you meet.

Most churches will be thoughtful enough to assist you in getting settled: helping unload, bringing food, cleaning the parsonage for you, inviting you to dinner, or answering your questions about your immediate needs. Thank the Lord if you find a congregation that is especially gracious and hospitable. If you do not, realize that you can help to teach them so that they may grow in these qualities and be better about them in the future.

A helpful text for your first sermon might be 2 Corinthians 4:5. It reads, "For we do not preach ourselves, but Jesus Christ as Lord, and ourselves as your servants for Jesus' sake." With such a message, you would demonstrate that you are not coming to preach your opinions, but Jesus Christ as Lord. You would demonstrate that you are there to serve, to help meet the needs of the people. Such an assurance would be welcomed by the congregation.

Stay Put

The first suggestion that P. H. Welshimer gives in his classic list (in Murch's *The Christian Minister's Manual*) is "Stay Put." This is good advice. A Bible college professor told his students, "Your first ministry or two will probably not be too long—perhaps just two or three years. But after you are out of school, plan for longer ministries."

Wayne B. Smith, minister of the Southland Christian Church in Lexington, Kentucky, told a seminary student that the most important suggestion he could give is to stay in one place for an extended length of time. He felt that the first three years are really just a "warm-up." The greatest work a preacher can do comes after that period.

Smith suggests, "If you are ever tempted to resign, wait a month before you do anything. If you still are convinced that you should resign, pray about it for a month. After that time if you are still sure, write your letter—but wait another month before turning it in." Most things that prompt a preacher to resign are relatively minor. After several months they may be seen in proper perspective.

The advantages of a longer ministry are many:

You know the people.
The people know you.
You know the community.
You have a good reputation both inside and outside the church.
You know what will work.
You know what won't work.
You know *who* will work!
You have demonstrated ability and stability.

Your Contract

The various parts of your contract should be worked out in interviews with the pulpit committee and/or board. Some congregations wish to have a written contract; others are opposed to one. If there is no written contract, be sure that the minutes of the board meeting and/or correspondence with the chairman of the board spell out in detail the matters upon which you have agreed. Once these matters are stated in writing, there will be no question about them in the future. At your next church, you may ask for similar (or improved) conditions.

Following are matters that should be specified in contract:

1. Beginning salary and the time at which the salary would be regularly reviewed (for example, once a year).
2. Housing allowance. It is advantageous for the minister to have a portion of his salary designated for housing expense. The Internal Revenue Service considers this nontaxable income. For more information, consult one of the tax guides for ministers.
3. Travel expense. When the minister uses his automobile on church business—calling, going to rallies, running errands—he should be reimbursed for his expenses.
4. Convention expense. This allows the minister to attend one or two conventions of his choice to help him perform his work better for the church.
5. Pension fund. Some type of retirement program should be instituted for the minister no later than at age thirty-five.
6. Medical insurance. Many churches will pay part or all of a medical insurance premium.
7. Social Security. Many churches pay the minister one-half of the self-employed rate to assist him in Social Security coverage.
8. Number of weeks vacation. This might be increased depending upon the number of years of service. Two weeks of paid vacation is usually considered a beginning place.
9. Attendance at conventions, retreats, and camps. Specify that these meetings are a part of the work of the minister and are not considered vacation time.
10. Time to conduct revivals. The minister might be allotted a certain amount of time for conducting revivals, away from the local church.

11. One day off each week.
12. Sick leave/disability arrangements.
13. Continuing education. Perhaps two weeks a year might be allotted for this purpose. Some churches pay part or all of the tuition.
14. Book allowance. Some churches give the minister financial assistance to help him build his personal library.
15. Arrangements for terminating the contract.

In the Appendix a sample contract is included. You might wish to secure copies of contracts used by other ministers to assist you in talking over contractual arrangements with a church.

To Go or Not to Go?

Eventually a minister will be contacted by another church, or it will seem evident that he should leave his present church for some other reason. The minister who wants to be used of God should not close his mind to the possibility of moving to a new congregation.

The amount of consideration given to an invitation will vary considerably. From the outset, some places and positions might seem unworkable. Past experience might dictate, for example, that one is better suited to work in a rural area than in the city. But there might be a city church where you could be happy and do your work well. Stewardship of time and talent might dictate an early negative response to a church in which you have no interest, or one that would drastically reduce your influence. Never use these offers to try to enhance your position with your present church, in order to bargain for a raise. Instead make your decision based on what you feel that God would have you do.

When you are contacted by a congregation, the representative may say, "We need a minister. Would you be interested in coming to our church?" It is quite proper to respond, "I'm very happy here. The work is going well. I don't have any plans to leave, but I am willing to consider the opportunity."

Generally a committee from that congregation would meet with you for an explanation of the possibilities. If you travel to their church, it is customary for them to cover your travel expenses. Frequently they will mention their willingness to do this when they first contact you. If they do not and if the church is some distance away, you might want to say, "With my schedule here, I would probably need to fly out and back. Would you be willing to absorb the travel cost if I were to come that way?" Usually they will respond, "We certainly will. We want you to come and see our area firsthand." If they do not make the offer, then you must decide whether you are interested enough to finance the trip on your own.

I have found it helpful to suggest to the representative, prior to such a meeting, that both the church and I consider it simply a matter of getting acquainted without any strings attached. If they decide that I am not the man for them, they would have no further obligation. If I do not feel that their church is the place for me, I would have made no commitment.

Frequently much general information can be exchanged by mail, so that one need not travel to a congregation in order to evaluate many facets of the work there. You might offer the leaders a copy of your resume, a summary report of your work with your present church, and other pertinent information. Often an annual report, a church paper, a bulletin, and a talk with one or two key leaders will give you a fairly good indication of whether you would feel comfortable with such a congregation. It is advisable not to visit a church unless you have a strong interest in going there, and even more advisable not to preach a "trial sermon" to a congregation unless you feel very strongly that this would be the place for you. A minister can easily get the reputation of one who is "always looking" but never willing to commit himself to make a move.

When a minister goes to "try out," he should stay for at least a weekend. An entire week is better, but is more difficult to arrange. His morning sermon might be a message typical of the sort that the congregation might expect of him on any Sunday. The evening message might outline his view of the work of a minister and examine some of the Biblical goals for any future relationship between them.

It is wise to avoid being a party to a "preacher parade." Churches that insist on bringing in several potential ministers, and then having the congregation pick a favorite, make the call of a minister little more than a popularity contest. This is not good for anyone and such invitations should always be turned down. Some churches include the following statement (or one like it) in their constitution.

In regard to a vacancy of the minister of the church, the elders shall serve as a pulpit committee. The committee shall investigate and recommend to the congregation applicants under consideration. After the applicant has had an opportunity to preach a trial sermon, the congregation shall vote on approval or disapproval. At no time will there be a competitive election.

A time may come when a minister feels that he needs to leave the church where he is serving, but does not have an offer from another congregation. It is possible to send a letter of application to a church that is looking for a preacher. While this is perfectly proper, it is to the preacher's advantage if the other church contacts him. He might ask a minister friend to indicate to a leader in the church that, "A friend of mine, Brother So-and-so, might be interested in making a change. I think that he is someone whom you would want to contact." If the contact can be made in this way, it is less awkward.

If you write a letter of application, keep it simple and brief. Outline your experience (or include a resume), note when you might be available, list references whom they could contact, and mention why you have particular interest in that congregation. State frankly, but modestly, your strong points. Offer to send further information, to talk with them by phone, or to come for a visit if they wish.

When you meet with the pulpit committee, it is good to have a list of subjects about which to ask. If they seem uncertain about the best procedure for the meeting, I have found it helpful to say, "Let me tell you a little about myself and then you can ask me any questions you have. I'll do my best to answer them. Then later on, I have some things I'd like to ask you about." You can summarize your experience and then respond to their questions. Eventually one of them will say, "I'm sure that you have some things you want to ask us." Then you can begin. A free, informal, give-and-take atmosphere is healthy.

Here are some of the subjects that you would want to cover:

1. How many are on your membership roll? How many are active? Where do they live in relation to the church? Where do they work?
2. Do you have a constitution and bylaws? Could I see copies of them?

3. How is attendance? (This is a leading question designed to bring up various problems and situations.)
4. Tell me about your problems of growth. What are you doing in local evangelism and missions? What do you want to do?
5. Tell me about your stewardship plans. How do you raise your money? What sort of budgeting do you use?
6. Tell me about your music and choir.
7. What do you expect of your minister? What would you see as the most important parts of my job, if I were to come?
8. What sort of relationship does the minister have with the elders and deacons?

If a minister has written a "philosophy of ministry" or has found one with which he agrees, he could give copies of this to the committee.

If a minister has certain convictions about the role of his wife as a member of the congregation, he should share these with the committee, too.

The prospective minister should be careful of questions like, "Does your wife play the organ?" or "Can your wife teach?" during an interview. He may assure the committee that his wife would be happy to assume the same type of role as any of their wives. Her first responsibility, however, is to be his wife and the mother of their children. She would attempt to work as any good woman in the church would work—but she would not hold any special place in the congregation because of her relationship to the minister. The interviewing committee does have the right to know anything about the minister's wife that might prove detrimental to the work of Christ at that church. They do not have the right to consider the minister's wife as an added unpaid worker whose services are guaranteed.

As You Leave

After a minister has been interviewed by a congregation, has preached a trial sermon, and has been approved by a vote of the congregation, then he is officially extended a "call" to that church. Some preachers have specified, "I will not come unless I get a certain percent of the votes." While I would never want to go without a substantial majority (ninety percent, for example), I have hesitated to make an arbitrary selection of such a number. I would rather weigh all of the circumstances after the vote and then prayerfully decide what I should do.

If the minister decides to leave, he should promptly notify the elders of his present congregation. It is inexcusable for them to learn from other sources that their preacher is leaving. Even if it seems advisable to delay a public announcement for a few weeks, the elders should know as soon as the decision is made. About two months' notice seems adequate; certainly not over three months should be expected. The contract should specify the length of notice required.

Rarely will a church ask the minister to leave. This ought not happen to you if you are sensitive to the feelings of the congregation and are working closely with the elders. But if this does happen, some ministers declare, "I'm not going to be forced out. I'll stay and fight," or "I'll start another congregation in the city."

It is hard to imagine a time that such a decision would be wise. Why would someone want to remain in an atmosphere of stress and friction when he had lost the confidence of a substantial part of the church's leadership? While starting new congregations is generally desirable, it is unhealthy to split a church and found a competing group. Often such a group has its chief loyalty to its preacher, its chief "enemy" those in the old church, and its chief accomplishment the defamation of the name of Jesus in the community.

Don't try to salve your conscience or save face by rallying your friends to your defense. It is wiser simply to leave and locate elsewhere. Leave as gracefully as possible. Seek to forgive. Your kindness will speak volumes and the cause of Christ can go forward there. If you are right and others are wrong, the truth will eventually be evident.

When his resignation is read to the congregation (usually at the close of a morning service), the minister can expect that it may be an emotion-filled time. He may wish to arrange for one of the elders to say a word of encouragement to the congregation after the letter is read, and dismiss them with prayer. This can relieve the minister of some pressure at that time.

A departing minister should not attempt to choose his successor. This is the responsibility of the congregation. He can answer questions about prospective candidates and even supply names, but he must avoid giving the impression that he is trying to handpick the man who will follow him. (Specific suggestions for his relation to his successor are included in Chapter 13.)

Supplementary Reading

Jay E. Adams, *Shepherding God's Flock*. Vol. 1, "The Pastoral Life."
Baker, 1975 (pp. 59-74).
Write for a catalog of material available from Church Management,
Inc., 411 Terrace Lane, Hopkins, MN 55343. Books and booklets
such as the following may be considered: *How to Pay Your Pastor
More; Pre-Parish Planner.*

Related Projects

1. Interview one or two ministers who have served in the same church
   for fifteen to twenty years. Ask them about times they were tempted
   to resign, why they didn't, and the values of a longer ministry.
2. Begin collecting sample contracts used by other ministers.

8

His Study

As you read, think about these questions:
—How can a minister begin developing a personal library?
—Other than books, what kinds of resources are available for a minister's study?
—What are the advantages of establishing regular hours for study at the church office?

James S. Stewart tells the story of a young minister who, concerned about the apparent failure of his preaching, consulted Dr. Joseph Parker in the vestry of the City Temple. His sermons, he complained, were encountering only apathy. Could Dr. Parker frankly tell him what was lacking?

" 'Suppose you preach me one of your sermons here and now,' said Parker; and his visitor, not without some trepidation, complied. When it was over, the Doctor told him to sit down. 'Young man,' he said, 'you asked me to be frank. I think I can tell you what is the matter. For the last half-hour you have been trying to get something out of your head instead of something into mine!' That distinction is crucial. Wrestle with your subject in the study, that there may be clarity in the pulpit."[1]

Great preachers are great students. If a preacher is to invite and hold the attention of a congregation, he must have something worthwhile to say and he must say it well. To do this requires effort. The discipline of personal study—in both formal and informal ways—is essential.

The Need for Study

Some are critical of higher education. One "self-educated" preacher was talking to some other ministers at a convention. "I'm thankful that I didn't go to one of them there preacher factories. That's all those Bible colleges are," he exclaimed. "All they do is crank out a bunch of preachers. They just give 'em a lot of book learning. Well, I'm telling you, fellows, I'm thankful for my ignorance."

One of the other preachers remarked quietly, "Apparently you have a lot to be thankful for."

We need to study. A man who had graduated from Bible college three years earlier said, "When I completed my undergraduate work, I was glad to get out of school. I didn't want to study any more. But after a few years, I found that I was running out of things to preach about. I decided that I needed to come back to school and study some more."

In the Warrack Lectures, James S. Stewart warned: "No minister of the Gospel has any right to cease to be a student when his college days are done. However burdened he may be in after years with the crowding cares of a large city congregation, however wearing to body, brain and spirit the toils of his twelve-hour day, he must and he can—by resolution, self-discipline, and the grace of God—remain a student to the end."[2]

The preacher has been compared to a man digging a well. He must go deeper so that he might have more to give to others. Continued study is necessary if one is to minister adequately. What minister thinks he knows all that he needs to know for his job? As he senses his inadequacy, he is motivated to undertake advanced studies.

Methods of Study

Study at its best is organized. A person might try to learn a little about a lot of subjects, but he should also attempt to learn a lot of the basics of Biblical knowledge. He needs to have the experience and guidance of those who have studied to help him. Many find that the discipline of classroom assignments is an excellent motivation for study. The basic requirement is that one plan to study and follow his plan.

One must make time available for study. The typical complaint of the modern preacher is that he has none, yet who is keeping him from study? Do his elders forbid him? Does someone lock up his books at 4:30 each afternoon? The man who does not study fails to do so because he has not made study time a priority.

Regularly occurring blocks of uninterrupted time are essential for study. As Homer A. Kent, Sr., advised, "The pastor needs to have *regular hours* for his study. Let the people of the congregation know what these are. If the people respect these hours, he will find it easier to keep them. Regular hours for study will be a great aid to the minister's efficiency."[3] These can be found at different times of the day for each individual.

Many ministers prefer the early morning hours for study. They are freshest then. They can think about the things they have read and discuss them during the day. Others prefer to read late at night, in the quietness of their home. (For those who have small children, the home may be anything but quiet!) The choice of study times is up to the individual.

One of the most helpful programs I have had is the practice of expository preaching. By going through Bible books, I am forced to study the Word afresh. I attempt to relate the Word to my preaching audience. I try to find fresh, lively illustrations that will relate to their lives. I know the people and their problems—I have probably just come from the hospital, or the funeral home, or a counseling session the day before. I find in the Word the answers to their needs. If one follows a program of preaching through the Bible, this will account for a large part of his study time.

The continuing student should read widely. He might need to increase his learning in certain general areas of human needs or problems; peace, love, God, guilt, and grace. He might read book reviews, to help him determine the best books available on a particular subject. He will want to consider both religious and general periodicals.

One of the dangers of relating study to preaching is that we may read the Bible only to help us with our sermons. This is tragic. We need times of personal communion with God and meditation on His Word to fit our own needs. I have found it helpful to read a book devotionally some weeks or months before I read it "exegetically" to preach from it.

Wise managers of time suggest that we should always have good books available. They can be at the office, at one's bedside, in the living room, or in the car. We can carry them with us into the doctor's office or onto the airplane. If we use the idle moments of the day to read, we can grow thereby.

The late Daniel Poling, longtime editor of *Christian Herald*, read at least one book a day. His prolific book review sections were an amazement to many readers. Poling read quickly, scanned frequently, but made good use of the time that was available.

We can learn in other ways, too. While we have emphasized the personal reading program of the minister, this is admittedly only one way in which he may develop. He should also counsel with other ministers. One of the rich blessings of my student-preaching days was a kind, experienced minister in a nearby town to whom I could go for counsel. He preached about twenty-five miles from where I did. I drove through his town on the way to the little community where I served. Frequently I stopped at his home. I always found him willing to listen to my problems and give practical suggestions to help me. Usually his wife fed me, too! He was a good friend—and the type of mature counselor whom every young preacher should seek out. The fledgling preacher would do well when around older ministers to heed James' advice, "Everyone should be quick to listen, slow to speak . . ."[4]

Frequently conventions, seminars, and lectureships are accessible to the minister. Various colleges and seminaries provide these special programs in addition to the many seminars now offered by other institutions and groups. Some preachers attend too many such gatherings. Still, they remain an excellent resource when properly selected and screened according to Scriptural principles. Many ministers find national brotherhood gatherings of special help, not only for their content, but because they provide the opportunity for fellowship.

Both formal and informal study groups are springing up. Membership in the Academy of Parish Clergy is open to all local preachers who want a supervised program of continuing study.[5]

As you might expect from one who has been dean of a seminary, I would not omit study for academic credit! Many educational institutions have arranged attractive schedules for those who can attend school only part time. Going on a two-days-a-week schedule—or just in the evenings—or every day over a short, concentrated period, one can continue his training under competent teachers. In some instances, extension classes are held away from the campus enabling even those ministers who do not live near a seminary to receive the benefits of professional guidance. Reading courses, correspondence classes, and credit for fieldwork experience are other alternatives in continuing education.

Most churches are willing to allow the minister time for graduate study. They realize that a good minister needs to study and that, by using the available opportunities, he can be guided by qualified professors, receive credit for his work, and have the motivation of classroom contact. Some churches are willing to pay all or part of the minister's educational expenses. Continuing education expenses for the ordained minister may be tax deductible.

Resources for Study

Your own library is a good place to start. It is not necessary to have a large number of books in order to have a good working library. Selection of books is of prime importance. One good book on a given subject will likely be sufficient for the young minister starting out. Basic reference works are also desirable. Bible translations are multiplying, but at least several of the more important ones should be on his shelf. Some churches give the minister an allowance to assist him in purchasing good books. Other preachers join book clubs, buy used books, and try in other ways to build a library "on a shoe-string."[6]

It may be helpful to put aside special income—such as from funerals or other speaking engagements—for the purpose of buying books. The cost of books, like other work-related expenses, should be carefully recorded and reported on his income tax form as a business expense of the minister.

Several lists have been compiled to show basic books that might be helpful in the preacher's library.[7] If a minister follows the practice of expository preaching through Bible books (see Chapter 15, Preaching), he will regularly add a good selection of commentaries on most books in the Bible.

He also has the resources of other libraries. Local libraries

often have a fair selection of books that a minister might need;
large city repositories have more. If the minister lives near a
Bible college or seminary, he may be able to borrow books
there. Some schools allow ministers to borrow books or tapes
by mail and keep them for a limited period of time.[8]

However he decides to do so, the minister must study! A
bishop visited a young preacher after the church service and
asked how the service went. He suggested that the preacher
might want to rest for a while, but the young man replied that
preaching never made him tired. The bishop answered, "Son,
whenever a man preaches, somebody gets tired." Listeners
learn quickly whether or not a speaker is prepared. The one
who has studied demonstrates to his congregation that he has
something worth saying.

The Place to Study

Ideally, the minister should have a place in the church
building where he can study. If a secretary is employed, her
office ought to be nearby so that she can screen visitors, take
telephone calls, and be available for dictation. If the minister
does not have a secretary, it is still wise to have a place to study
at the church.

When the minister must study at home, he should try to
arrange a private area where he will be as undisturbed as possible. His wife may function as a receptionist at times by answering telephone calls and welcoming visitors. This puts a strain
on her, however, because she has other duties, especially with
small children. It is difficult to find the quiet and solitude at
home that one needs for study. Yet it can be found! One may
study during the hours when the rest of the family is asleep and
callers are unlikely to come.

In the study, the minister should have all of his material
easily accessible. When he is at his desk, he should have his
most often used reference books, basic supplies, telephone, and
typewriter within reach. Chairs should be available for visitors
who come. The study should have adequate lighting and good
ventilation.

One of the finest challenges to study came from Floyd
Doud Shafer. Published initially in Christianity Today, it was
reprinted in pamphlet form—"Make Him a Minister of the
Word." Shafer says this:

Fling him into his office, tear the office sign from the door and nail on the sign: Study. Take him off the mailing list, lock him up with his books—get him all kinds of books—and his typewriter and his Bible. Slam him down on his knees before texts, broken hearts, the flippant lives of a superficial flock, and the Holy God. Force him to be the one man in our surfeited communities who knows about God. Throw him into the ring to box with God till he learns how short his arms are; engage him to wrestle with God all the night through. Let him come out only when he is bruised and beaten into being a blessing.

Set a time clock on him that will imprison him with thought and writing about God for 40 hours a week. Shut his garrulous mouth forever spouting "remarks" and stop his tongue always tripping lightly over everything non-essential. Require him to have something to say before he dare break silence. Bend his knees in the lonesome valley; fire him from the PTA and cancel his country club membership, burn his eyes with weary study, wreck his emotional poise with worry for God, and make him exchange his pious stance for a humble walk with God and man. Make him spend and be spent for the glory of God.[9]

If one is to preach the Word, he must know the Word. If one is to feed the sheep, he must have some food prepared. To be an effective minister, one must study.

Supplementary Reading

J. H. Jowett, *The Preacher—His Life and Work*. Harper & Bros., 1912 (especially Ch. 4).
Wilbur Smith, *The Minister in His Study*. Moody, 1973.
James S. Stewart, *Heralds of God*. Hodder and Stoughton, 1952 (especially Ch. 3).

Related Projects

1. Arrange a one-year study plan you might follow after you have completed your formal academic training and are spending full time on the field. Be sure to include books other than those that are directly related to your sermons.
2. Ask others for recommendations as you prepare a list of the ten most helpful books for a minister in each of the following fields:
   Preaching
   Counseling
   Administration
   Teaching methods
   Personal development

[1]Stewart, *Heralds of God,* pp. 123, 124
[2]*Ibid.,* p. 107
[3]Kent, *The Pastor and His Work,* p. 29
[4]James 1:19
[5]This non-denominational program will send information upon request (write to 3100 West Lake St., Minneapolis, MN 55416). The Society for the Continuing Education in Ministry is another such source (855 Locust St., Collegeville, PA 19426).
[6]Helpful advice is available in *The Minister's Library* by Cyril J. Barber.
[7]The *Seminary Review* published a practical basic book list in Vol. 25, No. 2. That issue can be obtained from The Cincinnati Bible Seminary bookstore, 2700 Glenway Ave., Cincinnati, OH 45204. Another bibliography is available for sale from Southwestern Baptist Theological Seminary, P.O. Box 22000, Fort Worth, TX 76122. It is called "Essential Books for the Christian Ministry."
[8]Tape libraries will lend cassette tapes to assist Christian workers. One such place is the Discipleship Tape Library, 435 West Boyd, Norman, OK 73069. Another is the Reigner Recording Library at Union Theological Seminary, Richmond, VA 23227.
[9]Shafer, "And Preach As You Go," copyright 1961, *Christianity Today.* Used by permission.

9

His Finances

As you read, think about these questions:
—What dangers are inherent in supplementing one's income with a part-time job unrelated to one's ministry?
—What are the advantages of the "housing allowance"?
—What expenses should be recorded for tax considerations?

His Income

A "paid ministry" is clearly taught in the New Testament. Proper support of those who give full time to preaching the gospel is basic in the church. "The worker deserves his wages."[1] "The Lord has commanded that those who preach the gospel should receive their living from the gospel."[2] No minister should be ashamed of receiving a reasonable salary.

We may expect our needs to be met. The problem comes in determining what is a *need* and what is a *luxury!* If we are honest, we must admit that most of us have not learned, like Paul, "to be content whatever the circumstances."[3] We know how to abound—but we don't always know how to be abased!

Despite the fact that the minister may never expect to be paid as much as other "professional men" in the community, the salary scale for preachers has risen substantially over the past twenty years.[4] Even when the salary is not what it should be, many ministers feel that the non-material rewards make up for it. They also believe that their work is a divine mission.

A minister and the congregation that hires him should have a clear agreement on his starting salary, the frequency of a "salary review," and by whom the review is to be made. Such fringe benefits as hospitalization insurance, retirement insurance, and Social Security payments should be agreed upon. The minister's business-related expenses should be considered separately from salary. His housing allowance should be arranged so as to provide the most advantageous tax consideration.

While his principal income will be from the church he serves, most ministers receive some additional income from weddings, funerals, other speaking engagements, or writing. Careful records must be kept so that all additional income may be accurately reported for income-tax purposes. One's expenses should also be clearly defined so as to receive every legitimate consideration from the Internal Revenue Service.

It is dangerous to plan a budget on the basis of projected, but uncommitted, income. Just because a preacher received $500.00 for conducting weddings one year, he cannot be sure that he will receive that much the following year. Therefore he should not plan to make car payments out of that extra $500.00! He might, however, decide to buy a new refrigerator at the end of the year, if he has received that much in additional income.

The temptation to take on other employment to "supplement" one's salary must be considered carefully. The legitimate supplementing of income can become an insatiable thirst for more and more. The desire for material things can easily draw a preacher from the pulpit.

If a minister begins some part-time job (unrelated to his ministry), his allegiance will be divided. Where will he give his best hours? What will he let slide? How will he ever live on a single income if he becomes dependent on something more? These considerations must be faced frankly and fairly when the minister considers outside employment.

This is not to say that a man may not be a "tentmaker," supporting himself so that a church which otherwise could not afford a preacher might have his services. It is to say that every preacher must remember the words of Jesus, "You cannot serve both God and Money."[5]

His Expenses

Most of us understand too well the saying: "There's too much month left at the end of the money." Where does it all go? We need to keep good records to find out! Obviously our first priority should be the money that we set aside for God. I would encourage every minister to give at least a tithe (ten percent) out of his gross salary before spending money for anything else. Taxes, Social Security, and other "payroll deductions" can come next. The Lord's money must never be siphoned off for some other cause outside of the church.

It is my conviction that a minister should give most of his tithe to the institution that employs him—whether it is a local church or a Bible college. He should not give all of it there, however. In addition to the local church, he will want to support the Bible college from which he graduated, missionary friends, and other worthwhile needs as he learns of them.

Savings should come next. Some banks suggest, "Pay yourself first every month." They mean by this that a man should put aside money regularly in savings before he begins to pay his other bills.[6]

Housing expenses are next in priority. For the minister, the government allows an excellent tax benefit. His parsonage (or housing allowance) is not considered taxable income. For this reason, it is important that all government regulations be carefully followed so that one may obtain the benefits Uncle Sam allows to ordained ministers.

If the church provides a parsonage and you pay certain expenses (such as utilities), ask that a part of your salary be labeled for housing expense so that these funds may be tax free. If the church does not provide a parsonage, ask that a portion of your salary be designated (before it is paid) as a "housing allowance." The amount should be approved in the minutes of the church board and properly labeled. This figure can include down payment, closing costs, monthly mortgage payments, utilities, insurance, and even furnishings. The amount set aside must be used—any unused portion is to be reported as taxable income. For specific details, one should consult current IRS guidelines and some of the ministers' annual tax guides.

The housing allowance is desirable for many reasons. It allows your family the opportunity to live wherever you wish. It allows you to build up equity. You can change the color of paint in a room without requiring a meeting of the board! The practice encourages stability and longer ministries. You will have a better understanding of the concerns that the other members have. The income-tax advantages that all home-owners have are even more dramatic for ministers. You may claim your interest as a deduction, as all do, but you are not required to report the amount labeled housing allowance as taxable income. You gain in two ways!

Automobile expenses should be carefully recorded. The minister may keep track of his actual mileage and claim the per mile cost allowed by IRS, or he may choose to keep track of all of his car expenses and take the percentage that represents the business mileage as his deduction. In any case, good records are essential.

The minister's food expenses will frequently include "entertaining." He might invite a guest for lunch to discuss church-related business. He may deduct such entertainment expenses for income-tax purposes if properly substantiated. The church itself should pay for specifically church-related meals that the minister purchases—such as for a visiting evangelist.

When the minister and his wife entertain a class in their home, the food expenses are also deductible as a part of his work. Similar tax deductions are available for books, office supplies, and other work related expenses. One should carefully follow all government regulations in establishing each deduction.

A part of his expense will be clothing. He needs to keep well groomed and up-to-date. This does not mean that he should be the first to adopt every new fad—but neither should he be the last one to leave an old habit!

Money should be set aside for continuing education. Seminaries frequently offer short-term (one-week) courses as a refresher or for continuing education. If you live near such a school, you might wish to go on a one-day-a-week basis. Correspondence classes and other innovative extension programs are available.

Good Money Management

1. *Keep good records.* Accurate financial records are a must. Not only are they crucial for IRS purposes, but they also

give you an appraisal of how much you have received and where it is going.

Payment by check is always safe. Your canceled check serves as a receipt. In gifts to the church, however, one should give through an offering envelope if possible. Your receipt from the church will then be accepted as verification of your gift, if your tax return is ever audited.

2. *Use a budget.* Several books provide basic assistance in budget planning (see resources listed at the end of the chapter). The entire family must cooperate in order to live within the terms of a budget.

One writer cautions: "Avoid amassing large debts. If a minister builds up a substantial debt and then moves to another work, he may leave behind large debts through no fault of his own. This can generate unfounded gossip directed against the church and make his successor's acceptance by the community more difficult. Arrangements should always be made with creditors when one moves away."[7]

3. *Ministerial discounts are occasionally offered.* If a merchant offers an unsolicited discount, the minister should accept the gesture with grace, while making it plain that he does not seek such financial favors. Unfortunately some go to the opposite extreme. One young lady is said to have bought some goods in a store and then asked if the firm gave a ministerial discount.

"Yes," was the reply. "Is your father a minister?"

"No."

"Your husband or your brother?"

"No."

"Why do you expect a ministerial discount then?" asked the clerk suspiciously.

"Well, you see," replied the young lady pensively, "I expect to become engaged to a Bible college student when he comes home next summer."

4. *Include insurance in your planning.* Your family can't afford to be without basic life insurance on the breadwinner. Term insurance can provide low-cost coverage while you are starting out. Whole life policies may be added later. These offer a cash reserve upon which you may borrow, in the event of a need. Automobile, health, and disability insurance should be added as funds permit. Some churches help pay for some of these coverages.

5. *Use good judgment.* Avoid "get-rich-quick" schemes. Be wary of financial ties to members of the congregation. Don't allow promoters to trade on your name (such as when one is promised a "kickback" for client referrals).

Supplemental Reading

John C. Banker, *Personal Finances for Ministers.* Westminster, 1973.
George M. Bowman, *How to Succeed With Your Money.* Moody, 1974.
Manfred Holck, Jr., *Making It on a Pastor's Pay.* Abingdon, 1974.

Related Projects

1. List the New Testament passages that teach a Christian about the proper attitude toward his possessions.
2. Keep a careful record of your income and expenses for one month. Then make a projected budget for the next year.
3. Study the requirements necessary to provide a tax-free housing allowance for the minister. Write up a sample motion that could be made to cover this in the board meeting. Estimate your total allowable housing expenses for the next year.
4. Begin keeping a record sheet for every category of business expense that is tax deductible.
5. Write to Minister's Life Resources, 3100 West Lake Street, Minneapolis, MN 55416. Ask for a free catalog of their money management materials. Their publication, *Seminary Quarterly,* is sent free to seminary students on request. They also publish a newsletter for ministers, *"Church and Clergy Finance."* Their booklet *Parsonage vs. Housing Allowance* surveys the pros and cons of a minister's owning his own house.

---

[1] Timothy 5:18
[2] 1 Corinthians 9:14
[3] Philippians 4:11
[4] A salary survey was conducted in 1977 by Glen Wheeler. The study considered typical salary arrangements for sixty respondents with wide variation in age, number of ministries, years of service, sizes of church, etc. The statistical information provided can help the young minister see what salary levels are typical. A profile based on the study appeared in *Christian Standard,* September 4, 1977.
[5] Matthew 6:24
[6] An excellent development of the principles outlined in this section can be found in *How to Succeed With Your Money* by George M. Bowman.
[7] Weed (ed.), *The Minister and His Work,* p. 24

Part Three

HIS RELATIONSHIPS

Section Outline

10. With the Elders and Deacons
    A. Biblical Guidelines
    B. Working Together
    C. The Board Meeting

11. With a Multiple Ministry
    A. The Secretary
    B. The Assistant
    C. Staff Relationships
    D. The Ideal

12. With the Community and the Church At Large
    A. With the Community
    B. With the Church At Large

13. With Other Ministers
    A. The Minister and His Predecessor
    B. The Minister and His Successor
    C. Other Ministers in the Area
    D. Guest Speakers

14. With Himself
    A. His Self Worth
    B. His Attitudes
    C. His Actions

10

With the Elders and Deacons

As you read, think about these questions:
—What does the Bible say about the relationships between the minister and the local church leaders?
—What are some "do's" and "don'ts" for introducing a new idea or program to the church leadership?
—In what situations is it best for a minister to assume leadership? In what situations should he remain in the background?
—What do church leaders expect of their minister?

The three important divisions of the local church are the preacher, the church leaders, and the congregation itself. In order for the church program to work smoothly, each one of these divisions must have confidence in the other two. If confidence is lost, difficulties will abound, and a change will have to be made unless it can be restored. This chapter deals with the relationships between the minister and the church leaders. By following the pattern and principles of Scripture, harmony between them can prevail, to the benefit of the church.

Biblical Guidelines

The elders are selected by the people and are answerable to them. (In some churches these elected leaders are called by

97

another name, but the same principles will apply.) Elders are
not infallible. They might make mistakes. A wrong man might
be put into office. Still, the church is responsible to follow the
leadership of the elders as long as they are elders. The congregation has recourse to remove a man who is unfit or unfaithful
through the election process.[1] One who should not be an elder
can be replaced.

The example of the New Testament is for a plurality of
elders to direct the affairs of the church. They are Scripturally
commissioned to "be shepherds of God's flock that is under
[their] care."[2] Elders are called overseers. They are to care for
God's church just as a man would manage his own household.[3]

While some use Titus 1:5 as a directive for the evangelist
alone to "appoint elders" in every town, surely proper interpre-
tation must consider the circumstances of the New Testament
church. An evangelist was not a dictator who arbitrarily
selected men for positions of leadership regardless of the feelings of the congregation.

That this was not the apostolic practice should be clear
from Acts 6. It became necessary for the apostles to appoint
men to distribute food, so that the apostles would be free to do
other tasks. They told the congregation: "Brothers, choose
seven men from among you who are known to be full of the
Spirit and wisdom. We will turn this responsibility over to
them . . ."[4] The multitude did the choosing, and the apostles
appointed them—that is, they set them apart to the work with
prayer and the laying on of hands. Even though in a new congregation the evangelist might suggest potential leaders to the
congregation, the Lord's people have a responsibility to select
those whom they are going to follow.

No minister should feel that he is above the authority of the
elders. The writer of Hebrews allowed no exception to their
rule: "Obey your leaders and submit to their authority. They
keep watch over you as men who must give an account."[5] The
minister, like every other member of the local congregation, is
under the oversight of the elders.

He is not, however, to be subservient like a slave to a
taskmaster. He might better be compared to an executive carrying out the policies of a board of directors. Naturally his counsel would be sought, his advice gratefully received, and his
experience appreciated. He is a part of the leadership team. In

some congregations, the minister is elected to serve as an elder, since he is expected to help shepherd the flock. Other congregations do not follow this practice. Neither arrangement is always the best.

When a preacher is contacted by the elders (they should be the pulpit committee), he can assess their ability and aptitude just as they will consider his. Complete honesty and trust should undergird every relationship of the minister and the elders. Nothing less is good enough.

Jay Adams stresses the importance of maintaining close relationships with the church leadership, particularly at the onset of one's ministry: "Probably the first most significant achievement of any minister who newly assumes the pastorate of any congregation is getting to know his elders well and learning how to function smoothly with them. No time can be invested more wisely during the first year of his pastorate (when, as a matter of fact, much else cannot be done anyway) than the time he spends developing and cultivating a close relationship to his elders. This, he should do, both individually and corporately."[6]

Adams goes on to warn that "It is important for the new minister not to discount his elders too quickly."[7] These men have lived in the community and worked with that congregation for some time. What may seem to be arbitrary or provincial on their part may well be the wisdom of experience. Here, as in other places, James' advice holds true: "Everyone should be quick to listen, slow to speak and slow to become angry."

Working Together

How does a minister get to know his elders? He should deliberately schedule time to be with each man individually. They might eat breakfast or lunch together, go calling together, or participate in some recreation. Retreats, special classes, prayer times, and other group activities should be encouraged also. Informal times of sharing build confidence and respect. A minister can almost anticipate an elder's reaction to a suggested plan if he knows him well. Familiarity with his elders also makes it possible for a minister to "try out" ideas privately before suggesting them in a formal meeting.

In most congregations, the minister is invited by the elders to attend and participate in their regular monthly meetings.

These elders' meetings would normally precede by at least a few days the "board meeting" to which the deacons are also invited. The preacher must be willing not to attend *every* elders' meeting. There are times when the elders will want to frankly and fully evaluate his performance, and he need not feel threatened or intimidated by such times. He might even deliberately plan another activity that would prevent his being at an elders' meeting, just to allow such ventilation of feelings on the part of the church leaders.

Most of the discussion in this section deals with the minister and the elders. The preacher also needs a similar close association with the deacons. The elders are the church leaders. They should make the primary decisions of the congregation (not simply "spiritual" matters). The deacons are helpers. They are to assist in the ministry of the church by fulfilling various duties assigned them by the elders. While this suggests a change from the actual practice in many congregations, there still can be monthly "board meetings" in which the elders and deacons share together with the preacher. These may be most helpful. In some churches, though, the deacons might outvote the elders if they wished at a board meeting. This ought not to be. The elders may report on decisions they have made to the deacons or, at other times, ask them to help decide a matter.

Adams suggests that a preacher might say something like this at his very first meeting with the elders: "Gentlemen, I am a sinner, and I shall fail. At times you will be disappointed in me as well as in other members of the congregation. I will need exhortation and help now and then, as indeed you will too. Therefore, you can expect me to be honest and straightforward with you. If I have any complaints or any concerns, you will hear them from me: you won't hear them first on the grapevine. And I expect to hear your concerns and your opinions directly, too. I shall not allow your honesty or your frankness with me to separate us. Rather, I shall always encourage it as I consider it essential to the adequate communication that is needed to bind us together. I will appreciate you all the more for your truthfulness. So come to me; don't go to anyone else, whenever you have a suggestion or complaint."[8]

As a minister, you will find it helpful to analyze the makeup of your church leadership (especially the elders). List the various vocations that are represented. Are there gaps or concentrations? It may well be that capable men from other backgrounds have been overlooked. If Scripturally qualified, they should be suggested to the congregation for consideration.

Next, list the ages of your board members. This is an enlightening practice. A church growth expert once warned me that, if nothing were done, I would eventually find that almost all of the elders and deacons were within ten years of my age. Until his warning, I had not realized that the new men we were adding were generally younger men—much closer to my age at that time. He stated that this can occur regardless of the age of the minister. It is a natural tendency, but one that must be guarded against.

The duties of the minister should be worked out in consultation with the elders. It is best to have some type of job description or written contract as one begins his ministry.

The minister is accountable to the elders. He will want to make regular reports to them. Such reports need not be overly detailed nor viewed as "how to measure what he is doing." Such judgments can be made and will be made on other things. Nevertheless the leadership should be kept informed both of the future plans and present work of the minister.

The elders should take particular concern for the well-being of the minister and his family. The minister and his family are the only members of the church who do not have a minister. They not only need the assurance that they can call upon someone for help when needed, but they require the attention that the personnel department of a good business bestows upon its workers.

Guy P. Leavitt noted that, in addition to the financial needs, "there are those little attentions which mean so much to all of us, such as recognition on our anniversaries or birthdays and gifts at Christmas, to mention a few. These little attentions have double value. They keep a minister happy, and a happy workman is the best workman. They also elevate the position of the minister in the eyes of the people so that they value his leadership."[9]

When a preacher comes to work with a new congregation, he must determine with the elders the priorities for the first year of his ministry. Normally the preacher will want to become familiar with the organizational procedure of the church and get well acquainted with the entire membership. He will naturally be contacting the "better prospects" at the same time. His wife will be getting acquainted with the women's activities of the church (not necessarily joining every group!) and both will get acquainted with the various adult Bible-school classes.

Normally the minister is a member *ex officio* of all committees within the church. He is not to oversee or "boss" any committee—but offer suggestions and comments. He can share in discussion like any other committee member.

You will find that it is much easier to get acquainted with people in small groups and in informal situations. Committee meetings, class parties, and other small group situations are extremely helpful for this reason. Inactive members and shut-ins should be contacted. The minister will want to get acquainted with the young people. In all of this, he must not neglect the elderly.

Does this seem like an impossible job? It is—if we set this as an absolute standard. If we view it as a goal, however, it is good. We must seek to keep balance—doing all that we can in each area. Then both God and the brethren will be pleased.

Do not attempt to make changes rapidly. Please underline that. Repeat it to yourself. Write it on a card and place it in a prominent spot on your desk. Many ministries have been weakened, shortened, or ruined because a preacher attempted to make rapid changes before he knew the people or had their confidence! In many cases it might have been before he even knew the situation!

A church leader once spoke at a national convention on the topic, "What I Expect of My Minister." He said that his minister should be a man committed to Christ who set a good example and who was willing to grow. He then pointed out that a preacher should take time to listen to what the elders and deacons are thinking, feeling, and saying: "Take another of those precious hours each week and schedule a one-hour session with each board member. It may take a year in some congregations but it will surprise you how stimulating and rewarding it will be for God's kingdom. What a chance to listen. What a chance to motivate! Explore 'in depth' what potential this 'sleeping giant' of a church board has. It not only will help you fight this partiality bug that sometimes bites us but each member must openly review his spiritual commitment and many will come away from that one-hour session a more determined steward of God."

The Board Meeting

In most congregations, the bylaws specify some regularity for meetings of the elders and deacons. Most common is a monthly combined session known as the board meeting. Some may call it a *bored* meeting, but this need not be.

The chairman is frequently the key for a good meeting. While the minister should not serve as chairman, he should work closely with him. The following suggestions should be discussed with the chairman of the board as plans are made for future meetings:

1. *The meeting should begin on time.* It is wise to set an ending time as well. If this is announced and carefully observed, it will increase attendance.

2. *Meetings should be governed by Robert's Rules of Order.* A member may be appointed by the chairman to act as parlimentarian. This does not mean that the session must be stiff and formal. On the contrary, a relaxed and comfortable atmosphere is desirable. Some boards serve coffee and donuts at each meeting.

3. *A printed agenda helps.* Such a sheet should be sent to every member a few days before the meeting, along with any recommendations or reports that will need to be acted upon. This in itself will speed up every meeting. (See the sample agenda in the Appendix.)

4. *A roll call is helpful for several reasons.* Not the least of them is that you may test a man's interest by watching his attendance over the year. Time should be given for devotions to help set the proper spirit for the meeting. Some boards have a brief (fifteen minute) instructional period prior to the start of the meeting with teaching on Biblical or practical subjects.

5. *Old and new business items should be handled in chronological sequence.* The minister should never suggest a "cold" proposition. A new proposal should be discussed with the committee and/or leaders involved long before it is introduced as business. Do not ask for a decision on any important matter until you know how it shall be put into effect. Decisions do not exist apart from their implementation.

6. *Every possible item should be referred to a committee for study and a recommendation.* This cuts down on long discussions when all of the facts are not available. When committees make reports, they should end with the words: "And we

move that this proposal be adopted and implemented." This immediately brings the suggestion to the floor in a proper way.

7. *Keep a good spirit in the meetings.* At one time I had a particularly cantankerous individual to work with in board meetings. I read through the book of Proverbs and copied down verses of Scripture that have helpful advice. I wrote these on a small card and kept it on the table before me (or in a file folder) during each meeting. The Scriptures were Proverbs 3:30; 10:12; 15:1; 17:14. They helped!

Supplemental Readings

Weldon Crossland, *Better Leaders for Your Church.* Abingdon, 1955.
Kenneth O. Gangel, *So You Want to Be a Leader!* Moody, 1974.
Gene A. Getz, *The Measure of a Man.* Regal, 1974.
W. R. Walker, *A Functioning Eldership.* Standard, 1942.

Related Projects

1. Talk to a minister who has participated in an elder/deacon clinic. Learn how it was set up, possible speakers, helpful resources, and how the program was first presented to the church leaders. Consider the possibility of such a training program in your congregation.
2. Review the resources available to you as possible training courses for the elders and deacons in your congregation.

---

[1] 1 Timothy 5:19, 20
[2] 1 Peter 5:2
[3] 1 Timothy 3:5
[4] Acts 6:3
[5] Hebrews 13:17
[6] Adams, *Pastoral Leadership,* p. 45
[7] *Ibid.*
[8] *Ibid.,* p. 47
[9] Leavitt, *How to Be a Better Church Officer,* p. 63

11

With a
Multiple Ministry

As you read, think about these questions:
—How can a good secretary assist in the total ministry of the church?
—What aspects of a minister-assistant relationship must be clearly defined if it is to work smoothly?
—What is the ideal in the relationships among staff members?
—What does it mean to "have your own church"?

A team spirit must characterize the multiple ministry. One man must be the quarterback and call the signals, but he is not a one-man team. Each member of the team must be assured that his intelligent and dedicated participation is essential for victory. If one fails to do his job, the goal may not be reached. The ideal state is reached when an older, more experienced minister and his young assistant, new to the ministry, can work together, side by side, to achieve the great goals of their ministry for Christ. This ideal is possible when they bear the proper relation to each other.

For a multiple ministry to be successful, each participant must have a proper attitude. This is not always the case. One senior minister with whom I worked as an assistant addressed letters to me as "Onesimus" and signed them "Philemon." Luckily he was joking!

Each staff member's job should be clearly defined. To

whom does he answer? From whom does he receive assignments? Does he have the authority as well as the responsibility to carry out his duties? While the elders will occasionally want to talk directly with the assistant minister or church secretary, they will normally communicate with them through the minister. Not every assistant needs to attend every board meeting. Good job descriptions and the wise matching of assignments to capabilities is a part of the secret of success.

For example, specific jobs for the assistant minister might be changed when a new person takes the position. One assistant may be especially talented in teaching, for example. He could handle a major part of the Wednesday night adult classes, while the senior minister assumes other responsibilities. The next assistant might not have the same talents and interests, so the preacher might assume a larger teaching load and ask the assistant to care for some of the other duties. In this way, each man can utilize his strong points and the work can be done more effectively. This principle applies to all church workers.

The addition of staff members does not minimize the need to use volunteer help by members of the congregation. It does mean that the equipping of the saints can be better carried on in most congregations with additional specialized leadership.

The Secretary

Church growth experts agree that the first paid staff member to be added after a preacher should be the secretary. She will relieve the minister of many routine duties and time-consuming details. This can free him to minister. In addition to having basic secretarial skills (typing, dictation, filing, etc.), she must also be able to function as a receptionist. She should be cordial, gracious, and patient.

A good secretary can answer fully half of the requests that come to a minister—whether by phone, letter, or in person. She can protect the minister's time and also keep him aware of concerns of various church members. A Sunday church bulletin, a weekly paper mailed to the home, letters to visitors, along with records of new, transferred, and inactive members—all may be a part of her work.

If the secretary serves a congregation that has more than one minister, it must be clearly understood from whom she is to receive assignments. Normally the minister will supervise her work while allowing opportunity for her to handle secretarial duties for other staff members at specified times. She is the church's secretary—not simply the preacher's.

The Assistant

What can be done to build good relations between a minister and an assistant?

1. A clear understanding of each man's authority, responsibility, and duties is basic. While the assistant is ultimately answerable to the elders, he is directly accountable to the senior minister who conveys their wishes to him.

2. Each must be loyal to the other. Senior and assistant must trust each other. Each will be able to serve some of the congregation more effectively than the other. This ought not to cause jealousy, but rejoicing. As long as the work goes forward, why should a senior minister be upset if the youth minister is especially appreciated by an older member of the church? Why not use that good relationship to help advance the cause of Christ rather than try to isolate the younger minister and view him as a threat to one's security?

3. The assistant must not be expected simply to "do the dirty work." While some of those jobs ("puttering piety") will be expected, the minister must do his share of the unpleasant tasks also.

While some ministers are accused of giving all the jobs they don't want to an assistant, others make the opposite mistake. They continue to do the unimportant tasks. Time management specialists maintain that the senior minister (or any chief executive) must stay away from the day-to-day operations, or he will have no time left for his real tasks of decision-making and planning for the future. Too many ministers have burdened themselves unnecessarily with small matters that can and should be handled by subordinates.

4. Each must be willing to learn from the other. A young minister may save himself many needless mistakes by listening to an experienced minister. Rehoboam did not heed the counsel of the older men and a rebellion by the people followed. Good advice is priceless.

5. Realize that you are partners. J. B. Phillips paraphrased Paul's advice like this: "Let us have real warm affection for one

another as between brothers, and a willingness to let the other man have the credit."[1] Such a relationship is essential for co-workers in a local church. Paul referred to his colleague as a "true yokefellow."

Staff Relationships

Richard Halverson, in an open letter to senior pastors, noted that some assistants felt alienated from the senior pastor and helpless to make any overtures toward reconciliation. He then described the mutual commitment shared by himself and his staff at Fourth Presbyterian Church in Washington, D.C.:

"We have an explicit commitment, first to Christ, then to spouse and family, then to one another, and to the officers and people of the church, in that order. We take our relationships seriously and practice fellowship on the basis of the formula found in Matthew 18:15-35. We treat alienation as intolerable, seek reconciliation as soon as possible when a breach occurs, and strive to maintain a loving, caring, affirming, supportive community."[2]

He noted that the associates have one full day each month to be together in worship, fellowship, sharing, and planning. Occasionally the staff will take an overnight trip together, including their spouses.

Weekly staff meetings are valuable. At one point in my ministry, I had three part-time assistants and two secretaries working with me in a church. One of the best times of the week was our Monday staff meeting. Occasionally my wife phoned while the meeting was going on and she declared that it sounded more like a party! There *was* some good natured fun—such as having a birthday cake for a staff member at the appropriate time! (Coffee and donuts were a normal part of the meeting.)

In the meeting we went over plans for the next few weeks and discussed future goals. Each member gave a brief report. Each of us had the chance to ask about any phase of the church program. We always included a time of devotion and prayer. A close-knit fellowship and an excellent team spirit developed. This is the way it should be.

Provide for each staff member's needs. Each needs to be provided with a private office. Even in churches without adequate office space, some classroom or other location may be used for a time in order to accommodate such an arrangement.

Help each person as he begins his work. The congregation needs to be clearly informed about the duties of each staff member. When a new person is added—particularly an assistant or secretary—it is imperative that a clear notice be given both orally and in the church paper that the person's work will be assigned by the minister (or whoever serves as his or her superior). This protects the new staff member from all sorts of requests that well-meaning members may make. (Such as— "We'll certainly expect you to be at our class meeting. Brother so-and-so always used to come." Or, "I know that you won't mind to run off 500 of these for the Boy Scouts; the former secretary helped us out this way all the time.")

The Ideal

Good relationships grow. They develop as each staff member demonstrates care, trust, and helpfulness to the others. Personality differences will naturally be present. One minister might not feel comfortable working with another. This does not necessarily mean that either is wrong, but only that this combination is not as compatible as others. Some men are "loners," and will do their best work outside of a multiple ministry.

The blessings of a team ministry can be many. When properly conducted, the team ministry provides for the church a model of discipleship and Christian community. Such an arrangement provides training for the younger, newer workers, and offers fresh insights for the older, experienced leaders. It also allows every staff member to have a day off each week and definite vacation time.

Each staff member has needs, just like other people. Psychologists identify at least four basic ones: recognition, security, opportunity, and belonging. When the staff and the total congregation understand that others have these needs and strive to meet them, the multiple ministry will succeed and the church will grow.

Ideally, each staff member should feel that he has his own ministry at his church, and is not just a part of someone else's ministry there. When Larry Hostetler resigned as an associate minister at First Christian Church in Phoenix, Arizona, to complete graduate study, someone asked him, "When you get your doctor's degree, are you going to get your own church?"

His considered reply was, "I have my own church."

In telling of the incident, senior minister W. S. Boice wrote: "Our brotherhood is rife with ministers who are afraid to share their ministry. The result is a truncated program, too often carried out by ministers ill-prepared by training or ability to get the work done which the church needs so desperately if it is to grow. Not every church needs to be large, but every congregation needs to be large of heart and tall of vision for the Lord."

Boice went on to explain how fortunate the congregation was to have four ministers there—all of whom "have their own church." He described the kind of relationships they enjoyed in their work together: "It is a shared ministry, not grudging, but happy. Each of the ministers has abilities and qualities the others may not have. Together, there is a strength and enjoyment no one could have apart. And best of all, it is both understood and shared by a great and growing congregation which is only beginning to make use of its great talents for the glory of God!"[3]

Supplemental Readings

Marvin Anderson, *Multiple Ministries—Staffing the Local Church.* Augsburg, 1965

W. L. Howse, *The Church Staff and Its Work.* Broadman, 1959.

Marvin T. Judy, *The Multiple Staff Ministry.* Abingdon, 1969.

Elam G. Wiest, *How to Organize Your Church Staff.* Revell, 1962.

Related Projects

1. Interview each member of the staff at two neighboring churches. Pick one congregation that seems to be growing and one that does not. On the basis of your interviews, attempt to assess what role the staff relationships play in the success or failure of a program.

2. If you are presently employed in a multiple ministry, invite the other staff members who work with you to read this chapter. Perhaps it could serve as a discussion starter for a sharing conference. "How can I help you do a better job?"—this should be the question that each would ask of the others.

[1]Romans 12:10, *J.B. Phillips'* translation
[2]Halverson, *Christianity Today,* May 23, 1975, pp. 41, 42
[3]Boice, article in *The First Christian,* August 1, 1973, p. 1

CHAPTER

12

With the Community and the Church At Large

As you read, think about these questions:
—What special privileges and responsibilities are placed on a minister because of his position in society?
—What are some arguments for and against participation in community organizations?
—How can one's ministry extend into the church at large, when his church is not part of a formal denominational organization?

The minister does not live in a vacuum. He lives in a community that in turn is part of a very real world. The preacher who isolates himself from his community cannot minister to many who need his help. He must wisely share his time and involvement beyond the local church.

With the Community

While his true citizenship is in Heaven, the minister is still a citizen of the place where he lives on earth. Our Lord recognized this in His answer to the question concerning taxation. One is never to render to Caesar what is God's, but he is to render that which is legitimately Caesar's. Paul declares that the Christian is subject to the "powers that be," since they have been ordained by God. When the minister registers, votes, signs a petition, or otherwise expresses his opinion (as an individual) on various issues, he is simply obeying the gospel.

The government recognizes the special position of the minister in today's society. He is normally exempted from jury duty and from service in the armed forces. The state will not and cannot force a minister to perform any service that violates his conscience and convictions.

While his position in society affords the minister certain privileges, it also places additional responsibilities upon him. He might be tempted to use his position of influence to promote a particular political candidate or issue. Naturally he will speak out for right and against wrong, but his involvement should not extend to the endorsement of political candidates or participation in similar partisan politics.

The obvious difficulty is for a minister to act independently as a Christian citizen and not to seem to speak in a quasi-official role for the church. When writing a letter to the editor, for example, he should use his home address and not church stationery. He is not writing as the minister of a church giving an "official" opinion, but as a citizen (who happens to be a Christian) who has an opinion that should be heard.

The minister will frequently be called upon to act as a "chaplain" by leading in prayer or devotions for P.T.A., civic, and fraternal meetings. Such participation may assist his work, providing the time is available and assuming that he will not seem to endorse wrong activity by his presence.

Participation in civic clubs is a similar issue. Some ministers ignore them completely—even to the extent of opposing their programs. Others become so involved in this type of work that their work with the church suffers drastically. Neither extreme is good. Although I have never been a member of a civic club (because of time limitations), I would not deny a brother minister that opportunity.

Of those who do participate, one is William Harold Hockley, minister at the Westwood-Cheviot Church of Christ in Cincinnati. He had served that congregation for twenty-four years before he became affiliated with the local Kiwanis club. Hockley states that he wishes he had done so long before he did. Membership in the club provided him contact with a number of business and community leaders to whom he could both witness and minister. Such a goal is a primary reason for a minister to participate in community organizations.

In all of his dealings in the community, the minister must remember that he is viewed as a man of God. Despite our abhorrence of a clergy/laity distinction, we must admit that it exists in the minds of most citizens. We must take this into consideration in our behavior.

Once I was in the bakery picking up an order. The lady who owned it said, "Here's your cake, Mr. Stone." She quickly caught herself and said, "I'm sorry. I should have said 'Reverend Stone,' shouldn't I?"

"No," I replied, "actually I don't use the title. Just Mr. Stone or Sam is fine."

"Oh, but you deserve it—you worked for it, I know!" she responded.

Her concept is a typical one for many denominations. What should I have done at that point? Would this have been the time to lecture her on the evils of a clergy system? Should I have quoted Psalm 111:9 and remind her that only God is reverend? I did not think so. I felt that it was better to be kind and understanding of her feelings and intent, while correcting what was wrong in her impression.

When the minister is seen in public, people notice if he gets mad, cuts in line, or honks at a slower driver. They think, "This man is supposed to be a minister of the gospel."

In small towns and rural areas, the minister's friendliness is especially important. One young preacher was asked by a congregation to resign because, as he walked to the post office each morning, he was always reading a book and did not speak to the people he passed on the street. Whether this is sufficient grounds for dismissing a minister may be debated, but it points up the importance that members place on the openness and friendliness of their preacher. One need not be extremely gregarious, but he must at least demonstrate common courtesy and Christian interest. Remember that two busy religious leaders completely ignored a man in need, but Jesus commended the good Samaritan who paused to help.

With the Church At Large

In recognition of the church in its broad sense, in a desire to avoid being provincial, and in an attempt to extend the cause of Christ, the minister must have an interest beyond his local congregation.

In free churches that have no denominational organization controlling them, it is especially important that such voluntary associations be accepted and carried out with a sense of commitment. The minister must have an interest in brotherhood life. Camps, benevolent associations, new church evangelism, conventions, Bible colleges, and other mission works will need his service. His willingness to give of himself in these ways (for which he might receive only an occasional meal or mileage check, if that) are a part of his ministry.

It is unfair for a church to send their young people to a Christian service camp when that congregation does not furnish any of the volunteer leadership for the camp program. It is not right to enroll our young people in a Bible college and never assist in the program of that school. It is not fitting that we should expect others to help plan the mission program or help arrange for a convention. Since there are many jobs outside the local church that we want to see done, we should be willing to help with them.

Along with this encouragement for interest and involvement in work beyond the local church, one caution should be given: keep your motives pure. Do not look on such participation as a way to get in good with the brotherhood leaders, or to get your name in print. Neither should it be seen as a chance to exert power and influence. Such concepts of success are directly opposed to the teaching of our Lord. Real success comes from obedience to Him through service to others.

Supplemental Readings

William Leach, *Handbook of Church Management* (chapters 18 and 21)
Ralph G. Turnbull, *A Minister's Obstacles*

Related Projects

1. Write out your definition of a successful minister. Is your goal a Scriptural one? How many of your activities are moving you toward that goal? What changes can you make to improve?
2. Talk with two ministers holding differing viewpoints on participation in community events. Which represents the better approach? What will your position be?
3. List the brotherhood organizations in which you have interest.

Which would you like to support or serve as a volunteer worker? What might you do to encourage others to share in these vital causes?

CHAPTER

13

With Other Ministers

As you read, think about these questions:
—What responsibilities does a new minister have toward his predecessor?
—What can be done by the departing minister to smooth the transition to the new minister?
—What problems can be associated with the transfer of members from a sister congregation in the area?

One's relationship with his peers deserves special consideration. Such relationships are crucial in any profession, but especially so in the case of a minister of the gospel. It is in his dealings with his associates that a minister frequently leaves himself open to criticism. Of these associations, perhaps his two most significant relationships are those with his predecessor and his successor in a congregation.

The Minister and His Predecessor

Respect him. Be big enough to rejoice at his worthy accomplishments and refuse to discuss his faults and failures. Learn from him. When you begin your ministry, study his methods and plans. Continue them as best you can, at least for a time. Do not attempt to make changes rapidly.

Don't be jealous of your predecessor. Don't permit yourself to be disturbed by the praise that members will give the former minister. A Methodist bishop once said, "Depreciation of a predecessor's deficiency ought to be as rare as it is reprehensible."

Naturally one would not do every single thing just the way the former minister did. There may be some policies and procedures that you will want to be assured *will* be changed even before you accept a call. There may be other things that the elders would not want you to do as the previous minister did. They will probably tell you what they feel should be done differently. A congregation will normally accept changes if they are for the better, if you don't make them too rapidly, and if you don't make too many of them!

A minister can acquaint himself with his new church by reading over the minutes of the previous five years' board meetings. In this way he can come to understand some of the feelings and attitudes of the church leadership and the congregation. He can learn of programs that were tried, but proved unsuccessful. If he wants to institute a similar program, he can be sure to call it by a different name than the previous effort that failed.

It is helpful to write or phone the former minister (even before he leaves the congregation, if possible) to ask for his suggestions and ideas. A frank, understanding, friendly visit can be helpful to everyone. Normally you could write or phone him soon after you have accepted the call. In situations where the former minister is leaving due to a severe problem, such a contact may not prove advisable.

When the former preacher returns for a visit, the new minister will want to call on him and make him feel welcome. He may be invited to preach or participate in some way at the services.

When I began work as associate minister at one church, one of the older deacons stopped by to shake my hand on the first Sunday. He began telling me how much they thought of the former associate. He bragged on him. He praised him. "There will never be another one like him," was the message that came across.

Later I talked to the senior minister about it. He said, "Don't worry! He'll feel just the same way about you in a little while." And he did! Members must be allowed to love more than one minister. Don't expect ties of friendship and fellow-ship that had been established by years of happy associations with your predecessor to end just because you have come to a church. They can't and they shouldn't. Accept the fact that the members loved your predecessor, then love them in such a way that they will love you, too.

The Minister and His Successor

As soon as a minister resigns, he must begin to prepare the way for the one who is to follow him. He can do this in his letter of resignation, by indicating his confidence in the future of the church. He might assure the congregation that God will assist the leaders in locating the right man to preach there after he is gone.

Do everything possible to help make it easy for the man who follows you. You might spend two or three of your last messages dealing with the subject of transition. Preach on "the work of the minister" and remind the congregation of the Bib-lical perspectives. Give practical suggestions for ways that they can help him. Everyone will know that you have nothing to gain personally by offering these suggestions, but are only in-terested in helping the church.

The congregation should be reminded to expect changes in personality and style. You might tell them something like this: "Don't expect the new minister to be just like I am. I wasn't just like the preacher before me—and he wasn't just like the preacher before him. We are all different. He is not coming to fill my shoes any more than I could fill the shoes of my pre-decessor. Each man must fill his own shoes. He may do some things differently than I. Let him try his own ideas. Work with him. Support him—just like you did me." Such conditioning will help prepare the flock for the new minister. You may want to remind the people again of the Scriptural premise that, "One sows, another waters, but God gives the increase."[1]

Give him all possible assistance. As soon as your successor is chosen, write him a warm letter of congratulations. Assure him of your desire to help him in every way possible. He may have questions. Attempt to answer them fully and frankly.

For the last month or two that you are there, begin compil-ing any information that the new minister might need. You may wish to write out a general evaluation of the state of the work, as you see it. You might also include reminders on various special duties that the minister is expected to handle, upcoming events that he needs to begin planning, and special notes about current programs. Unfinished projects and goals not yet achieved could also be listed. Leave an accurate, up-to-date list of the church members with addresses and telephone numbers; also go through the prospect list and leave it as up-to-date as possible. Let him know about area ministers' meetings (when, where, and whom to ask about information). Tell him about future revivals that are scheduled. You may wish even to suggest doctors, places for auto repairs, or anything else that might help him and his family make the transition to their new residence.

There are limits to how much information the new minister should be given. Take care not to bias him for or against any individual or group in the congregation. One writer has wisely suggested, "A new preacher should be told much, but not everything. Give the people a chance as well as the preacher!" Jay Adams issues a similar warning: "Leave nothing prejudicial (for or against) *any* individual. If such matters are that *crucial,* they should be handled before leaving (at least brought before the attention of the elders, who, rather than the departing minister, can inform the next pastor if the situation continues). Nothing potentially slanderous may be left."[2]

After you are gone, don't return too soon. Stay out of his way. Give the new preacher time to get his feet on the ground. Don't try to keep a "hold" on the people—writing to them, phoning them, stopping by, inviting them to come see you. It is natural for you to want their attention. One's ego will not be fed as fully in the new situation. You will miss the love that you felt there. But remember that the new minister is just as unsettled as you are and he deserves a chance to get started on his own.

Bishop Warren A. Candler of the Methodist Episcopal Church, South, once spoke to some young ministers. He referred to the question that they were soon to answer: "Will you go where you are sent and that gladly and willingly?" Bishop Candler said he should like to make this, "Will you go where you are sent and stay away from where you've been?" He added, "Now John Wesley didn't put that last part in, but if he had known what I know he would have."

The congregation can learn to love *both* of you, but give

them time to make the adjustment. If you do, you'll find that everyone will get along better.

Occasionally church members criticize the new preacher. You do not have to encourage or support this. Instead defend him, if possible, even though you might do things differently. Don't ever be placed in a situation that will put you in the role of opposing or downgrading your successor. When you return to the city, phone him or stop by to see him. Pass along compliments about him that you may have heard. Let him know that you are on his side.

As a rule, it is best to announce before you leave that you will not plan to return for weddings and funerals. Occasionally there may be a special request from a family. Ask them to have the present minister contact you about it. Indicate that you feel he should also participate in the service if you were to come. In this way, you will demonstrate that you are not trying to undercut his work in any way. In an interim period between ministers, there is no problem in returning to assist.

In his helpful volume in the "Shepherding God's Flock" series, Jay Adams suggests that when one is asked to return for a wedding, he might write to the member, along with his thanks, "I make it a policy usually not to return to do this, since I think it's a transgression of the care and discipline of the new minister. Is there any special reason for the request beyond the great joy that it would give to both of us?" He suggests that a copy then be sent to the new preacher with a note such as, "Joe, do you really think that there is any good reason beyond sentiment for me to return to conduct this wedding, or would you rather do it yourself?"[3]

Other Ministers in the Area

Get acquainted quickly with preachers in sister congregations in the area. They will be of inestimable help as you get acquainted with the community and its customs and peculiarities. You may find special friends among these brethren, with whom you and your family can relax.

Ministers of other religious groups should also be greeted as time permits. You will find occasions when you may work together on projects of community good. These men can also assist you with information concerning newspaper publicity, hospital parking, and other practical details. Opportunities to share one's convictions about New Testament Christianity are also available.

Friendships with ministers of other groups can be valuable and enriching, whether or not you agree on all details of their doctrinal position: "We need the fellowship of other pastors. The pastorate is a difficult work, and God's servants can help to hold one another's arms up as we fight the battle together. We recognize the fact that there is a vast difference between acquaintanceship, friendship, and fellowship: and that having a cup of coffee with a pastor friend is not quite the same as asking him to preach in your pulpit. You will find men in your area who may not agree with you on every detail of theology, but whose fellowship will enrich your life and ministry. Get to know them; pray for them; pray with them. Major on the important facets of the faith, not the minor things. Learn to listen and you will learn from them."[4]

In cities where there are other churches of like faith, it is particularly important that the minister must refrain from giving any hint of proselyting. It is unethical to visit a member of a sister church and encourage him to change his membership to your congregation. If such a person begins attending your services, send a note of greeting to him. If he continues to come, phone the minister of his church and say, "What's the story on this family? They've been attending our services for the last few weeks." Frequently the other minister will say, "They became unhappy about some situation here. We tried to resolve the problem, but had no success. I am glad that they are going to your church. Why don't you call on them and see if they can be enlisted there?"

Some years ago a minister remarked wryly, "I don't think that our churches in this city really grow—they just exchange disgruntled members!" When people become dissatisfied in a congregation and seek another place to worship, you will want to welcome them, but without taking sides against a brother minister. You ought not to seek such people, however, and you should view them with caution. Those who became upset with another preacher might also become upset with you!

Guest Speakers

When another minister is invited to speak at your church, a number of guidelines should be followed. The elders should approve all who preach or teach there. Such approval should be secured before a formal invitation is issued. This will avoid embarrassing situations that can arise.

If the contact is originally made by telephone, be sure to send a letter spelling out the arrangements, by way of confirmation. The following details should be covered:

The date and time (be sure to note any change in time zones)

Location of the meeting

Type and size of audience expected

Length of time allotted for message

Financial arrangements

Housing arrangements

Meal arrangements

Material needed for publicity

Title and text of message if needed (and when you need it)

Telephone numbers by which the preacher (or the contact person) can be reached

When an evangelist comes for a revival, it is proper to ask his preference concerning meals. Most evangelists would prefer only one large meal a day. If one eats in homes for two meals a day, this becomes a problem. Some preachers prefer to eat before the evening service, while others would rather eat afterward.

Arrange a private place for the speaker to stay. If a motel room does not seem preferable, find a home where he might have privacy. To "avoid the appearance of evil," do not choose a household in which the husband works and would leave the evangelist there alone with the man's wife for a large portion of time.

Be sure that the honorarium is ready to present to the speaker after the session. When he is flying in from a great distance, it is thoughtful to offer to send reimbursement for his air fare in advance. A personal note of appreciation can be mailed to him soon after the meeting.

Supplemental Readings

Sam E. Stone, "You and the New Minister," *Christian Standard*, Nov. 20, 1977, pp. 9, 10.
Sugden & Wiersbe, *When Pastors Wonder How*. Moody, 1973.

Related Projects

1. List all of the information which a minister should leave for his successor. Compare your list with that of Jay Adams (*The Pastoral Life*, p. 70).
2. Ask two or three ministers how their predecessors have helped them in starting a new ministry.

---

[1] 1 Corinthians 3:5-9
[2] Adams, *The Pastoral Life*, p. 70
[3] *Ibid.*
[4] Sugden and Wiersbe, *When Pastors Wonder How*, p. 114

14

With Himself

As you read, think about these questions:
—What temptations are unique to those in the ministry?
—How does the apostle Paul exemplify a minister with a proper attitude toward himself and his work?
—What can a minister do to help himself in his work and his personal life?

What other career can equal the potential for good that is available to the Christian minister? Not only has he many opportunities to serve others, but his career also provides him with the largest field possible for the growth of his own soul. Yet many preachers admit to discouragement and disillusionment.

Why does this happen? The rich soil that will produce a fine garden will also nourish destructive weeds. Temptations and trials will accompany the preacher. He will be tempted to be self-righteous, to seek popularity, to use people rather than serve them. His association with holy things can make them seem common to him. Unless a minister loves the Lord with all his heart and sees himself in a proper relationship to God, danger is ahead.

The apostle Paul is one of the finest examples of a Christian worker who "had it all together." Nowhere do we get a more intimate look at the man himself than in his letter to the Philippians. Let me suggest three areas of the minister's personal life for consideration, based primarily on that epistle.

His Self Worth

Love yourself. Paul noted that he *could* boast on human grounds, if that were his choice.[1] While he did not "put confidence in the flesh," he realized that (humanly speaking) he could have. He was aware of his strong points. He was aware of his capabilities, his talents, his good experiences. Yet Paul was humble.

To be humble, one need not think little of himself; he simply must not think of himself at all. In C. S. Lewis' *The Screwtape Letters*, a young demon is advised by his more experienced Uncle Screwtape how best to tempt and befuddle his human "patient." In one of my favorite passages, humility is discussed:

> You must then conceal from the patient the true end of Humility. Let him think of it not as self-forgetfulness but as a certain kind of opinion (namely, a low opinion) of his own talents and character. Some talents, I gather, he really has. Fix in his mind the idea that humility consists in trying to believe those talents to be less valuable than he believes them to be. No doubt they *are* in fact less valuable than he believes, but that is not the point. The great thing is to make him value an opinion for some quality other than truth, thus introducing an element of dishonesty and make-believe into the heart of what otherwise threatens to become a virtue. By this method thousands of humans have been brought to think that humility means pretty women trying to believe they are ugly and clever men trying to believe they are fools. . . . The Enemy [Jesus] wants to bring the man to a state of mind in which he could design the best cathedral in the world, and know it to be the best and rejoice in the fact, without being any more (or less) or otherwise glad at having done it than he would if it had been done by another.[2]

Our Lord commanded, "Love your neighbor as yourself." If we are to love others properly, we must love ourselves. Self love is not wrong—unless it assumes improper proportions. It cannot come before our love for God and it must be accompanied by love for others. If a man loves his life more than God, he will lose his soul. But if a man loves God, loves himself (the person that God is helping him become), and loves others, he can live a healthy, happy life.

Take care of yourself. Your body needs proper rest and care. It is not selfish to take care of what God has given you.

I have never forgotten what a good friend told me years ago. He mentioned how some people live by the adage, "I'd rather wear out than rust out." Then he added, "I've found that those are not the only two alternatives. You can take care of the machinery, give it some oil, and it will work a lot better and last a lot longer." Amen! The minister who drives himself, never takes a vacation, and is constantly short of sleep, behind schedule, and overworked may feel that he is a martyr when he achieves his heart attack at forty-two, but I'm not sure God views it that way.

Take time off. One day of rest per week is not just a union bargaining point, but a Scriptural principle. Vacations are also essential. Everything looks different when you are rested and refreshed.

When you are ill, go to the doctor. Don't try to push on and do more than is wise. Preventive medicine (such as a yearly checkup) often saves money as well as your health.

Don't ever make a major decision when you are sick. Billy Graham has stated that this principle has saved him from some tragic mistakes that he otherwise might have made in his ministry. Physical problems can affect your emotions and even your thinking. Keep the right balance and take care of yourself.

Know yourself. "A balance must be maintained between the minister's self-image and his duties ... the minister must build (or be building) a bridge between his own inner reality and the outer reality of what others expect of him and what he actually does."[3]

How does one achieve such a balance? Not by trying to follow a man-made set of rules ordered for him, no matter what man is doing the prescribing. No single set of rules can account for all the differences among individual people. One works toward achieving the balance by getting to know himself—physically, emotionally, and in other ways—and by fitting his strengths and weaknesses into a viable style of his ministry.

Assess your interests. Discover your talents. Learn when you can do the best work. Find the ways in which you minister most effectively. Do not be afraid or ashamed to acknowledge these abilities frankly but humbly.

Protect yourself. A minister's reputation is his stock in trade. He must never give his name to an organization or movement to which he cannot give his time and attention. He must not allow others to use him. His name is not a piece of merchandise. His reputation must be guarded always.

A friend told Plato of a terrible change that had been leveled against him. Knowing it was not true, his friend said, "What are we going to do?"

Plato replied, "We must simply live in such a way that people will know it is false."

There will always be someone who will suspect something, criticize something, or think something evil of you. You must seek to live above reproach. "Avoid every kind of evil." Demonstrate by your life that you are living for the Lord.

Be yourself. No facade is necessary or desirable. The minister may be tempted to build his ego by identifying himself with all the "good" he does in the church as a result of his ministry. But this is just the opposite of how his self-image should grow. The minister should do good as an outgrowth of a fulfilled and fulfilling life with Jesus Christ.

Think of the people that you like. Aren't they the ones who admit their shortcomings, acknowledge their weaknesses, and are open and honest to all? They do not have to run themselves down in order to be open and honest.

You are someone special to God. You mean something to His kingdom. Never forget your self worth.

His Attitudes

Despite his confinement in a prison cell, Paul remained content. His attitude was right. He declared, "I have learned to be content whatever the circumstances. I know what it is to be in need, and I know what it is to have plenty. I have learned the secret of being content in any and every situation, whether well fed or hungry, whether living in plenty or in want."[4]

His attitudes are further revealed by the many expressions of joy that flavor the short Philippian letter. His optimism is illustrated by his view of his imprisonment. Even though he was in jail, he could see that God was bringing good out of it. Although his preacher enemies were trying to make life miserable for him, he thanked God that Christ was being preached. What a lesson! When the preacher must deal with a board member whose motives are unworthy, but who works for God, he can take a lesson from Paul.

The thought life of a Christian minister is the key to his success or failure. Freud said, "Thought is action in rehearsal." It is hard to imagine that any minister ever committed adultery without first committing it in his heart. Jesus said, "As a man thinks in his heart, so is he." He knew the danger of bad thoughts and called men to purity of mind.

If a man is to be what God wants him to be, then he must think godly thoughts. Temptations will come—but he need not harbor them in his mind. To Martin Luther is attributed this famous quotation: "I may not be able to stop a bird from lighting in my hair, but I certainly can stop her from building a nest there." Can the minister afford to fill his time with suggestive stories from the television screen, paperback books, and movies? Can he saturate his mind with worldly music? What is his conversation usually about? The apostle Paul told the Philippians, "Finally, brothers, whatever is true, whatever is noble, whatever is right, whatever is pure, whatever is lovely, whatever is admirable—if anything is excellent or praiseworthy—think about such things."[5]

The apostle also wrote to his Philippian brethren, "Do not be anxious about anything, but in everything, by prayer and petition, with thanksgiving, present your requests to God."[6] Not worry, but prayer, is the Christian's solution. Bishop Quayle tells of a sleepless night when he was concerned about a problem in his church. Finally, in the wee hours of the morning, he said he felt as if the Lord had put His hand on his shoulder and said,"Quayle, you go on to bed. I'll stay up the rest of the night!" We need the quiet confidence that comes when we turn our worries, fears, and anxieties over to the Lord. He can keep us in perfect peace—if we keep our minds on him.

Every minister will have times when he feels that he is not appreciated, that he has not been treated fairly, and that his church is the most difficult field in the world. Expect these visitors—but don't let them become permanent residents. "Set your minds on things above, not on earthly things."[7] You will need the reassurance of a sympathetic listener at times. Your wife can help, but she should not be your only confidant. Perhaps a brother minister in a nearby community would be a good "sounding board." Don't keep all of your frustrations to yourself. Find ways to work them out. Some do so by athletics, others by gardening or music. Find your way.

When we have times of despair and depression, we need

the same treatment that the Lord gave to Elijah. The Lord told him to take care of his body—through rest and proper food and drink. He demonstrated His power so that Elijah knew that he need not depend on his own strength. Elijah then went on to serve. A similar confidence is demonstrated by the apostle Paul: "I can do everything through him who gives me strength."[8]

Such attitudes are, ultimately, a more important asset for a minister than any particular ability he might have. In his book, *The Measure of a Man*, Gene Getz used as an example Paul's teaching on the qualifications of an elder: "There is very little reference to an ability or a skill. Rather, out of the twenty qualifications listed, nineteen have to do with a man's reputation, ethics, morality, temperament, habits, spiritual and psychological maturity. And the other one has to do with his ability to lead his own family. . . . I would much rather work with a man who is qualified spiritually and psychologically than one who has lots of skill and is yet carnal. A man who has the qualities set forth by the apostle Paul can quickly develop skills and use them for the glory of God." He goes on to discuss the implications of such standards for a church seeking a "qualified" minister: "Judgments are often made on how well he can preach or teach, and not what he is as a man, which has frequently led to tragic consequences."[9]

His Actions

Christian attitudes are impossible to maintain apart from Christian actions. In Philippians, Paul makes it plain that the Christian is to be distinguished by his way of life. He says, "Whatever happens, conduct yourselves in a manner worthy of the gospel of Christ."[10] He also writes, "Do everything without complaining or arguing, so that you may become blameless and pure, children of God without fault in a crooked and depraved generation, in which you shine like stars in the universe."[11] One's outward conduct and manner of living speaks volumes about the kind of person he is inwardly:

> You tell what you are by the friends you seek,
> By the very manner in which you speak,
> By the way you employ your leisure time,
> By the use you make of dollar and dime.

You tell what you are by the things you wear,
By the spirit in which your burdens you bear,
By the kind of things at which you laugh,
By the records you play on the phonograph.

You tell what you are by the way you walk,
By the things of which you delight to talk,
By the manner in which you bear defeat,
By so simple a thing as how you eat.

By the books you choose from the well-filled shelf;
In these ways, and more, you tell on yourself.
                                   —Author Unknown

Paul's letter to the Philippians reminds us that not all ministers have a concern for other people: "Everyone looks out for his own interests, not those of Jesus Christ."[12] But Paul urged Christians to imitate Christ in their dealings with others: "Do nothing out of selfish ambition or vain conceit, but in humility consider others better than yourselves. Each of you should look not only to your own interests, but also to the interests of others."[13] And Paul practiced his own principles—he prayed for the Philippian church; he was concerned for them; he sought to help meet their needs.

While every Christian should demonstrate such concern, people demand a higher standard from the minister than from others, whether we like it or not. The self-centered, thoughtless preacher is attractive to no one. His work demands something better. The preacher must care about others. He will quickly be labeled a calloused professional if members see that he does not really listen when they talk to him or come when they need him.

While his concern for others is important, so is the manner in which the minister conducts his dealings with others. "Conscious that he is the representative of Christ and His church, the minister should look, speak, act, and live the part," the late James D. Murch advised ministers. "Gentle and affable manners are essential. Emerson says, 'A beautiful behavior is better than a beautiful form—it is the finest of the fine arts.' Rudeness in manner and coarseness in speech must be avoided. Kind words, smiles and good deeds; deference to authority; condescension to the lowly—these are some of the marks of the man of God." The poise of a well-groomed servant of God enhances the effectiveness of his message. "Noble carriage is important.

It will require effort to stand straight, walk erect, and be impressive in form and movement, but it will add weight and force to one's message."[14]

The Christian minister should also be well-groomed and dressed in such a way as to make him acceptable in the community in which he lives. He should strive to look proper and correct for the occasion. Formal dress is often correct, but not at all times. Informal dress can make him look more like a part of his community, but not at all times. He should avoid extremes in style that would tend to make him stand out.

The minister must also take care of his body. While the maxim "cleanliness is next to godliness" does not happen to be in the Bible, it certainly applies to those who would communicate the gospel to others. Frequently those who have bad breath and body odor do not seem to be aware of it. Ask a friend. Ask your wife. Do your part to be clean and neat always.

The minister who desires to take good care of the "temple of the Holy Spirit" will also be careful about diet and exercise. The temptation to let one's stomach be his god did not end with those of whom Paul spoke in Philippians 3:19. A few ministers have even been known to overeat!

Exercise is also advisable. Fit the program of exercise to your age and to your needs; it should be worked out in consultation with your doctor. Be careful about the once-a-year strenuous activity of camp when it is preceded (and followed) by inactivity.

The Christian minister's actions are most important because they will lead to his own salvation or condemnation. A preacher might say all the right things, appear at all the correct places, and act respectably and with "Christian" decorum. Therefore, people assume, he has no personal spiritual needs. But the minister himself knows better. He must, above all else, be sure that he himself is right with God. Only the continuing struggle for honest personal faith will eliminate the "holy masquerade."[15]

To Paul, this meant more than everything else. He advised the Philippians, "Continue to work out your salvation with fear and trembling, for it is God who works in you to will and to act according to his good purpose."[16] As ministers, we will not be all that we ought to be. We will not be all that we could be. But we must resolve to make every effort to be what Christ wants us to be. With His help, we can do better. Without it, we will surely fail. Paul sums up his advice in his triumphant declaration, "I can do everything through him who gives me strength."

Supplemental Readings

Wayne Oates, *Confessions of a Workaholic*. World, 1971.

Wayne Oates, *The Minister's Own Mental Health*. Channel Press, 1961.

Samuel Southard, *Pastoral Authority and Personal Relationships*. Abingdon, 1969.

Related Projects

1. Take a personality test from a trained counselor. Discuss the findings as they relate to your work. Become aware of other testing resources for counseling use. (Write for information to Family Life Publications Inc., Box 427, Sazuda, NC 28773.)
2. Discuss some of your frustrations and concerns with two other ministers—one older than you and one about your age.

---

[1] Philippians 3:4-14

[2] From *The Screwtape Letters* by C. S. Lewis, pp. 72, 73. Copyright © C. S. Lewis, 1942. Used by permission of the Macmillan Publishing Co., Inc.

[3] Weed (ed.), *The Minister and His Work*, p. 30

[4] Philippians 4:11, 12

[5] Philippians 4:8

[6] Philippians 4:6

[7] Colossians 3:2

[8] Philippians 4:13

[9] Getz, *The Measure of a Man*, pp. 17, 18

[10] Philippians 1:27

[11] Philippians 2:14, 15

[12] Philippians 2:21

[13] Philippians 2:3, 4

[14] Murch, *The Christian Minister's Manual*, p. 13

[15] Weed, *op. cit.*, pp. 29, 30

[16] Philippians 2:12, 13

Part Four

HIS JOB

Section Outline

15. Preaching
    A. The Importance of Preaching
    B. The Type of Preaching
    C. A Plan for Preaching
    D. Improving Your Preaching
    E. The Goal of Preaching
    F. The Preacher Teaches

16. Counseling
    A. Need
    B. Limitations
    C. Development of a Program

17. Administration
    A. A Biblical Basis
    B. A Necessary Function
    C. A Crucial Task

18. Motivation
    A. Your Attitude
    B. Your Influence
    C. Your Awareness
    D. Your Results

19. Calling
    A. Types of Calls
       • Prospects
       • Members
    B. A Calling Program
       • Sources of prospects
       • The cultivation process
       • Involving others
    C. Principles for Calling

20. Conducting Services
    A. The Worship Service
    B. Baptism
       • The prerequisites
       • The preparation
       • The service itself
    C. Weddings
       • Whom will you marry?
       • What conditions will you set?
       • What preparations should you make?
       • What of the wedding itself?
    D. Funerals

21. Implementing the Program
    A. The Committee System
    B. Organizational Requirements
    C. New Members
    D. Attendance Record
    E. Christian Service Interest Sheets
    F. Recruiting Workers
    G. Church Files
       • Members
       • Non-members
       • Church
       • Office records
       • Minister's personal records

CHAPTER

15

Preaching

As you read, think about these questions:
—How does preaching contribute to the rest of one's ministry?
—What are some of the advantages (and demands) of preaching "through the Bible"?
—What qualities are necessary to good preaching?
—What kinds of teaching opportunities are open to the minister?

The Importance of Preaching

As in every other part of life, Jesus remains our example for the work of the minister. A study of Jesus' ministry reveals how important preaching was to Him. Knofel Staton, professor at Ozark Bible College, cited the evidence from Christ's ministry: "Did Jesus believe in preaching? He surely did! When He got back to His hometown synagogue after His baptism, He declared: 'The spirit of the Lord is upon Me, because He anointed Me to preach the gospel to the poor. . . .' (Luke 4:18) All of His other activities were to come after preaching."[1] Our Lord's emphasis on the spoken word merits careful consideration.

Although a minister has many duties to perform in his work, preaching remains primary among these. Preaching can increase his opportunities to minister to people in other ways; it can provide motivation and encouragement for other kinds of work done by the minister and the congregation in general.

135

Richard Brown, minister and Bible college professor, noted the importance of both counseling and evangelism in one's ministry, but found preaching to be supportive to them both: "The counseling minister will find his counseling opportunities diminishing if he cannot hold a congregation together on Sunday. The most energetic evangelistic program will fail if those who are brought into the fellowship of the body of Christ find it to be a corpse. I believe in preaching!"

The reverse of this process is also true for the Christian minister. Not only does his preaching strengthen all other aspects of his work, but these in turn provide him with resources for his preaching. The minister sees many people throughout the week, and he knows their needs. He cares about them. He wants to help them. His job gives him a rich variety of experiences from which to draw material for his sermons: experience of God himself, and knowledge gained from study and from his work and fellowship with other people.

As Staton concluded in his article, "The Priority of Preaching," "May more of us be able to echo the words of Jesus, 'I must preach . . .' (Luke 4:43) and the words of Paul, 'Whether then it was I or they, so we preach and so you believed' (1 Corinthians 15:11). And may the whole world be able to say before Jesus returns, 'Indeed we have had good news preached to us' (Hebrews 4:2)."[2]

The Type of Preaching

The man who believes God's Word will want to explain it to others. For him, how can there be any doubt that Bible preaching is the best kind? In our time, we have seen a new-found emphasis on Bible preaching taking place. Tragically, too many of us have remained followers in this movement when we should be in the forefront, even though we claim to be a Bible-believing people.

The tragedy is that in many churches the pulpit is weak, shallow, and ineffective. This is not because the minister is a theological liberal, but because, even though he is "true to the Bible," he says so little. Too often he is not willing to put forth the effort in study and preparation required for genuine Biblical preaching. At a preaching workshop, church growth specialist Paul Benjamin criticized this tendency: "Sermonizing requires thinking, and, as someone has pointed out: 5 percent of the people think; 5 percent of the people think that they think; and the other 90 percent would rather die than think! . . . Some of these ministers who have a natural aversion to thinking anyway simply give up the time-battle and preach the sermons of other men. The apostles, of course, were at a decided disadvantage at this point since James S. Stewart, Clovis G. Chappell, Clarence E. McCartney, Herschel H. Hobbs, J. Wallace Hamilton and Billy Graham hadn't written their sermons yet!"

If we as preachers have only our own opinions to deliver, what right do we have to claim the attention of several hundred people for a half hour every week? If we are only serving a warmed over version of some sermon book message, why not simply sell copies of the book and let the people stay home? If we are doing nothing more than parroting popular cliches, why did we spend years in Bible college and seminary study?

The best alternative, according to many pulpit giants, is the use of expository preaching. Such messages are good for the people and for the preacher as well. Harold Knott, in his classic work on the subject, defines an *expository sermon* as "an attempt to explain, illustrate, and apply the Scriptures to life."[3] An expository sermon need not be dull or lengthy. The preacher need not discuss every commentator's view on every word. Certainly he need not go verse-by-verse through an entire chapter in one message. True exposition breathes the very life of God into a gasping, dying world. It revives! It renews life! It meets the practical, pertinent, pressing needs of men.

Dr. John W. Montgomery insists that all genuine preaching is expository preaching. The minister must attempt to explain and interpret the Biblical text, and this places certain demands on him: "Every preacher must be an exegete, and the more he exegetes, the more genuinely he preaches. If the Word of God is the true source of the preacher's insights, he must expound it; but to expound it, he must understand it; and since it comes to him in written language, he must analyze it linguistically. Here there is no substitute for knowledge of the original languages of the Scripture."[4] A minister must be well enough acquainted with Greek and Hebrew to look up a word in the lexicon and be sure of the original meaning without having to rely on the translator or a commentator. He must also be familiar with the other tools of study that are available.

If preaching isn't the most important thing in your ministry, it ought to be. If your preaching is not *Biblical* preaching, it ought to be. The man who wants to preach God's Word must study the Book. He must read it, memorize it, and share it. He must love it. He must want to be a Bible preacher. The job is not easy, but neither is it impossible.[5]

A Plan for Preaching

That pulpit master F. B. Meyer defined expository preaching as "the consecutive treatment of some book or extended portion of Scripture on which the preacher has concentrated head and heart, brain and brawn; over which he has thought and wept and prayed, until it has yielded up its inner secret and the spirit of it has passed into his spirit."[6] His definition tells us two facts about this type of preaching: first, it demands continuous, exhaustive work; second, it follows a Scriptural sequence. As such, expository preaching lends itself well to a general plan for preaching.

Harold Ockenga explained how he used expository preaching almost exclusively in his ministry:

> For five and one half years of my Pittsburgh ministry I preached through book after book of the New Testament—John's Gospel, Acts, Romans, I and II Corinthians, Galatians—all on Sunday morning. Truly, since this was my first major effort on this line, it was limited; but I was trying my wings to reach the proper stride or level of my gifts. By the time I began my ministry in Park Street in 1936, I was primarily an expository preacher. Hence, I began at Matthew 1:1 and in twenty-two years have preached through the entire New Testament at my Sunday morning and Friday evening meetings.[7]

If a minister wants to begin preaching expository messages according to a plan, he first chooses the book or books that he feels will best meet particular needs within his congregation. He estimates the number of weeks that should be devoted to each study—depending on how much material he expects to cover each week. He may decide, for example, to preach a series on the minor prophets during morning worship for the first thirteen weeks in the fall. He might begin, at the same time, a six-month series on the book of Acts in the evening services. Dates for revival meetings, faith-promise rallies, or guest speakers can all be taken into account by the original plan. He may also wish occasionally to interrupt the series to deliver a special message relating to some crucial event or important occasion.

For a lifetime of personal and congregational growth, a definite plan of expository preaching will be highly effective and appreciated—not easy, but worth the effort! Among the advantages of a plan of expository preaching are the following:

It is Biblical. When properly followed, expository preaching is sure to be true to the message of the entire Bible. Not only does it deal with every great theme of Scripture, but it grants them consideration proportionate to the space allotted them by divine intention.

It permits variety. Sermons may be biographical or textual, for example, and still be expository. An expository sermon can be recognized by the fact that it is based on a passage of Scripture—whether the emphasis is on one verse or many.

It is satisfying. A minister cannot help but be encouraged when he brings God's message and watches it help people.

It is enriching, both for the preacher and the congregation. People want and need Bible exposition; it will help build churches. The minister himself has a feeling of accomplishment, at having preached through an entire New Testament book. He will always feel more at home with that part of the Scripture and will be able to interpret it more accurately.

It helps you plan ahead in your work. With a long-range plan for preaching, you know far in advance the books and topics you'll be preaching on. You can buy books and take special classes to help you in dealing with that particular Biblical book.

It provides a supply of sermon topics that will never run out. When I began to preach an older minister told me, "I don't know what I would do if I had to think of a topic every Sunday. I know I would run dry in a hurry. I don't see how a preacher can stay fresh and creative unless he practices expository preaching."

Expository preaching does cost, however.

It costs disciplined study to determine the author's meaning of a passage as revealed by the context of that passage and by the original language. If you are skilled in Greek this may be easy for you. It is not for me.

It costs dollars to buy commentaries and studies for the book at hand. Popular sermon books may be less expensive.

It takes time to divide a book into units of thought that are each suitable for a message.

It is not easy to discuss some of the topics that come up.

It may challenge your own opinions on the church today and on your role within it.

It demands an agonizing, constant search to find pertinent illustrations to enrich and enliven your presentations. You need humor, poetry, modern-life stories, Biblical background, anecdotes—all of the ingredients that go into any good sermon. And you must find the ones that fit this passage!

It costs you sleep when you know that you must produce a sermon on the already-announced passage of Scripture for the next Sunday! That sermon barrel never looks so good as it does when it is off limits!

Improving Your Preaching

What Hemingway said of writers is equally true of preachers: "All of us are apprentices in a craft where no one becomes a master." No amount of experience ever qualifies a minister to neglect the work of improving his presentations.

Plan ahead. Planning is the key to success. A minister would be wise to follow some plan for preaching like the one proposed in the previous section. Many ministers like to arrange a general sermon plan for one year in advance. They might make a projection during the summer, to be started on September 1. Some ministers have two sequences of sermons planned, one for morning and one for evening services. Some ministers like to follow quarterly cycles in conjunction with the Bible-school curriculum.

Once your basic program is planned for the year ahead, you may arrange file folders in which to collect material, notes, ideas, and suggestions for your sermon outline.

Prepare carefully. W. H. Griffith Thomas reminds us that, after deciding upon the text or topic, "We must think ourselves empty, read ourselves full, write ourselves clear, pray ourselves keen."[8]

As you read the Bible book from which you will preach, go through it first slowly without other aids. Note major divisions of thought as you see them. Note recurring themes. Then divide the book into workable sections suitable for messages of normal length. In my own case, I refuse to read a commentary or sermon book before going over the text in this way so that I may develop at least the outline and thrust of the sermon on my own.

Read the book again and again, including new and fresh translations. Read the finest commentaries. Watch for illustrative material in all of your other reading. If one begins preparation for a series of messages well in advance, all of his reading, conversation, and study can be directed to seek out interesting illustrative material.

File folders or envelopes are good to use in gathering material for the sermon. A file folder is especially handy because it is easily opened and can contain all of the notes, references, and the finished product. Some ministers list the places where the sermon was used (and the date) on the outside of the folder or envelope. I keep such a record on a card file where the messages are arranged by title. Then the sermons themselves are in file folders and are arranged by text. Topical messages are kept in a separate drawer by title. Occasionally one will find a Scripture passage, quotation, or idea that will fit into a previous sermon as well as a future one. These can then be easily incorporated into the appropriate file folder.

Begin early. Good time management is especially crucial in sermon preparation. As a Bible college student, I was overwhelmed by the advice, "A minister should spend one hour in his study for every one minute he is in the pulpit." I decided that my sermons would need to be quite a bit shorter than they had been! While I cannot always claim to follow this guideline, I do commend it as an excellent plan. It points up the necessity of careful and thorough preparation.

Start early each week, and early each day. Establish deadlines for the completion of your sermons, and stick to them. An attainable goal would be to have both Sunday messages finished before the weekend. Do not try to complete most of a week's work on Saturday afternoon. Not only will you be frustrated, but the quality of your sermon will suffer.

One method of getting ahead of schedule in one's sermon preparation is available to the minister who is preaching through a book. He can do all of his preliminary study on a larger section of Scripture than the one he intends to preach from. That way, he can get ahead for the following few weeks.

Have variety. According to one speech expert, "Listeners

want enough novelty to offset monotony just as they want enough familiarity to maintain stability." Some of the newer forms of pulpit address, such as dialogue preaching, can be used with success. Having an occasional guest speaker also enriches the spiritual diet of the congregation.

Relate properly. To be a Biblical preacher, one must present God's message in an understandable, interesting manner. Some ministers appear to use big words in an effort to appear scholarly or sophisticated. Instead, they come across as pompous or ponderous. Billy Graham once criticized this tendency among some preachers: "Some of you think that Jesus said, 'Feed my giraffes.' He didn't. He said, 'Feed my sheep.' You must not put the food above their heads!"

Martin Luther is reported to have said, "When I preach in the *stadtkirche* I stoop down. I do not look up to the Doctors and the Masters of Arts, of whom there are about forty in my audience, but I look upon the crowd of young people, children, and servants, of whom there are several hundreds. To them I preach. To them I adapt myself. They need it. If the Doctors don't care to hear that style of preaching, the door is open for them to leave." What a lesson for those who feel that to be profound they must be polysyllabic!

As you write your sermon, visualize the congregation. This will help you to eliminate the irrelevant and clarify your ideas. Keep personal forms of address. Translate abstractions into concrete terms. Remember that you are preparing a sermon, not a lecture, term paper, or essay.

Illustrate effectively. Illustrations have been compared to the windows of a house. They are there to let in light, and they also break up the monotony of a wall. You might not want to live in a house made up completely of windows, but neither would you want one without any at all.

Do not take refuge in ready-made collections of illustrations. The illustrations of others cannot possibly fit your particular subject, style, and personality as well as the illustrations you find yourself. Far better are those that come to you in the course of your own activities, conversation, and reading. The discovery of such illustrations is more exciting than simply looking them up in an anthology. When you are thinking about a certain subject for an upcoming sermon, you will be surprised how many instances in your daily life seem to relate to that subject—more than you had noticed before you started thinking about your sermon. Be ready for them. Cultivate the habit of carrying note cards with you wherever you go, for the purpose of jotting down pertinent ideas while they are still fresh in your mind (old roll call cards are excellent!).

Good illustrations are hard to find, but don't give up looking for them. One strong, fitting illustration is better than many that are obscure, irrelevant, or borrowed secondhand.

Stop when you are through. Some preachers are like a pilot circling the landing field. They head down and get ready to land, but suddenly rev up the motor and take off again.

This reluctance to conclude one's message can cause members to feel like a certain stranger who entered church late. As he was taking his seat, the sermon was already in progress. Soon he began to fidget nervously. "How long has he been preaching?" he whispered to the man in front of him.

"Oh, about thirty or forty years," was the reply.

"I'll stay, then," he said. "He must be almost through."

A sermon need not be eternal to be immortal. You will find that your audience becomes restless if your message lasts more than twenty-five to thirty minutes.

The Goal of Preaching

In the vestry of a church in Scotland hangs a sign, that a minister sees just before the enters the pulpit. It says: "No man can bear witness to Christ and to himself at the same time. No man can give the impression that he himself is clever and that Christ is mighty to save." We must preach so as to point men to Jesus and His Word. We must hide behind the cross.

Look at the men who have reached the most for Christ, built the largest churches, written the most popular books, and composed the hymns and gospel songs that have lasted over the years. They were not trying to impress people with how many big words they knew—they were simply trying to communicate Christ's truth. Their knowledge was used to direct people to Jesus Christ in the most compelling way they could. Cold, distant scholarship will not motivate or inspire people. A storm of emotion may have temporary effect, but it does not really help or teach people. Appeals to both the mind and the heart are best.

A well-known minister told about a misconception he once had about preaching: "I thought that an evangelist couldn't read and a Bible scholar couldn't preach. Later I found that there was another alternative. You could combine zeal with knowledge!" He's right. The ideal preacher is one who can think with the philosopher and the theologian, but communicate in the language of the common man.

Edwin V. Hayden identified the primary goal of preaching in this way: "Let experience, reason, and imagination provide the decoration that adds interest and attractiveness to the sermon; but never rest on experience, reason, or imagination for argument, teaching, or essential application. . . . Let the weight of all these structural elements rest squarely on a clear 'thus saith the Lord!' To do otherwise is to build for ultimate collapse; it is to preach divisive doctrines; it is to raise a foolish challenge against the sole authority of God's Son. Preach the Word!"

The Preacher Teaches

Our Lord's final directive commanded His apostles to preach *and* teach, yet many ministers have excluded themselves from this latter area of potential ministry. As James D. Murch observed, "Even in these modern days there are altogether too many ministers who devote themselves exclusively to preaching and draw a line between the ministerial work of the church and the educational work of the church school. Yet it is generally conceded that the minister who is most successful and whose influence is widest in teaching the Word and building character has a great church school 'used as a field to be reaching, then as a force to be worked.' "[9]

Heralding the message of salvation need not be confined to the pulpit. The most effective minister will both preach and teach. Any arbitrary line drawn between preaching and teaching seems inadequate. They are two different, but not exclusive, methods of presenting the same revealed truth. Good preaching will include teaching. Good teaching will frequently include exhortation, often associated with preaching.

A minister will teach those who are unsaved, both in classes ("How to Become a Christian") and at home. At the same time he will help instruct believers in Christian living. He might teach a "Now That I'm a Christian" class for new members. Wednesday night training sessions, Saturday evening classes, home Bible studies, and other teaching opportunities are available. Some preachers are able to teach a Bible-school class in addition to speaking in the worship service. Others find this difficult, particularly if they are involved in multiple Sunday morning worship services.

By teaching in the Bible school, the minister strengthens it, according to P. H. Welshimer. The Bible school can widen the area of service available to the minister, while at the same time bring him closer to individual members of the congregation: "By virtue of the fact that he teaches in the school he gives it dignity. Here he can find opportunity to do his best work. It is heart-to-heart work. In the pulpit he may be far removed from his audience; in the Bible class never."[10]

Recognizing the importance of good communication is essential. While profundity is fine, obscurity isn't. C. S. Lewis once suggested, "An essential part of the ordination exam ought to be a passage from some recognized theological work set for translation into vulgar English. . . . Failure on this paper should mean failure on the whole examination."[11] Teaching isn't complete until the pupil has learned what the instructor is attempting to teach him.

The minister must be closely involved in the selection of appropriate curriculum material for the entire church program. Even when an education minister is employed, the preacher must be aware of what is being used. Dr. Larry Richards notes that suitable curriculum "seeks to raise the student's level of Bible learning . . . reflects an awareness of the gaps that block response to God . . . and good lessons reflect the writer's awareness of structural factors that help create the desire to learn."[12] Not only the theology, but also the teaching methods of the curriculum must be examined.

While the minister does not have the time to devote to teach every individual in his congregation, he can make sure that careful teaching is being done. He can disciple leaders to handle various teaching responsibilities. In all of his teaching efforts, he is to follow the apostolic command, "The things you have heard me say . . . entrust to reliable men who will also be qualified to teach others."[13]

The minister who has teaching ability must develop and use that gift for the kingdom. He will do well to find a place of service where his co-workers have talents that are complementary to his. The minister who feels that he has little ability to teach can still develop his talents as far as possible. He can become acquainted with the basic principles of Christian education while he encourages others to assume leadership in this field. It is impossible, however, for an effective minister to be completely divorced from the teaching program of the church.

Supplemental Readings

Harold E. Knott, *How to Prepare a Sermon*. Christian Restoration Association, 1977.

Harold E. Knott, *How to Prepare an Expository Sermon*. Christian Restoration Association, 1977.

Lloyd Perry, *A Manual for Biblical Preaching*. Baker, 1965.

Merrill Unger, *Principles of Expository Preaching*. Zondervan, 1973.

Related Projects

1. Interview two of the best preachers you know. Ask them about their resources, their planning, their problems, and their joys.
2. Write out a three-month plan for sermons for both morning and evening services. Let one be an expository series.

---

[1]Staton, "The Priority of Preaching," *Christian Standard*, June 5, 1977, p. 9

[2]*Ibid.*, p. 10

[3]Knott, *How to Prepare an Expository Sermon*, p. 11

[4]Montgomery, "An Exhortation to Exhorters," *Christianity Today*, March 16, 1973

[5]Various objections to expository preaching are dealt with in my article, "For Pulpit and for Pew," *Christian Standard*, June 15, 1968, pp. 5, 6. Evidence is given to show that expository preaching does not cause a decline in attendance, but brings response to the gospel invitation and is appreciated by the people.

[6]Quoted by Knott, *op. cit.*, p. 11

[7]Ockenga, "How to Prepare a Sermon," *Christianity Today*, October 13, 1958, pp. 10-12

[8]Whitesell, *The Art of Biblical Preaching*, p. 68

[9]Murch, *Christian Education in the Local Church*, pp. 215, 216

[10]Quoted by Murch, *Ibid.*, pp. 219, 220

[11]Quoted by Kennedy, *The Seven Worlds of the Minister*, p. 169

[12]Richards, *Creative Bible Teaching*, p. 141

[13]2 Timothy 2:2

CHAPTER

16

Counseling

As you read, think about these questions:
—What qualities must a good counselor have?
—How far should a minister go when he counsels someone? At what
  point should he refer the person to a professional counselor?
—What factors should govern the establishment of office hours that
  the minister makes available for counseling?
—What kinds of counseling is the minister expected to do?

When Paul told Timothy to "preach the Word," he added
that he should "correct, rebuke and encourage—with great patience and careful instruction."[1] Such concern for the
individual—to help him mature as a Christian person—is the
work of a counselor. The minister will often be called on to talk
individually with those having serious problems and facing
grave decisions. Loving concern for others must characterize
the man of God.

Gerald Kennedy has declared, "We must always be pastors
before we can be prophets . . . I can think of no instance where a
man combined these two worlds of his calling, that he did not
find success and joy in all his work."[2] With the increasing
number of family problems being referred to the minister for
assistance, no survey of his work can fail to touch on this as-
pect.

Need

Jay Adams stresses the importance of counseling in one's ministry: "Counseling is a work that every minister may, indeed must, perform as a faithful shepherd of Jesus Christ. He must plan to do counseling, must learn how to do counseling and must make himself available for counseling."[3] The minister will find that he is expected to assist in all types of situations. Some of these will seem totally beyond his preparation and ability. In such cases, he may refer the individual to a competent psychologist, psychiatrist, or other Christian counselor. On such occasions he may assist the person by going with him on his first visit to the psychiatrist.

Adams is opposed to counseling centers and non-Christian therapists: "Referral, except to another faithful shepherd, is out of the question. Better than referral is personal growth on the part of the pastor through discovering and ministering God's answer to the problems encountered in pastoral counseling."[4] Both time limitations and the nature of a minister's gifts prevent an absolute acceptance of Adams' view.

Fortunately in a growing number of communities, capable Christian counselors are available. These individuals combine Christian faith with a background in psychology to equip them to minister more effectively to the needs of individuals. Other ministers in the area can help you locate such a person.

Despite the availability of qualified professional counselors, the effective minister must be able to do at least basic counseling himself. He can begin by being open and receptive to the needs of others. He can listen. He can show that he cares. He can teach what God's Word says. While not every minister feels skilled in counseling, every minister can be a loving, accepting, and caring person. As he does these things, he can help others solve their problems.

In discussing the symbolic role of the pastor, Wayne Oates noted Paul's description of his pastoral function as that of an ambassador. We represent God's Word and show His will to those who need to know it: "The careful, intelligent, and devoted management of the unique interpersonal relationship of the pastor to an individual or group becomes the normative definition of pastoral care and personal counseling. As such, the pastoral task is the participation in the "divine-human encounter.""[5]

The church is the only authentic healing community that there is. Any Christian can listen to someone and love him. The minister is often the first line of defense for those who have emotional difficulties and trials. He must be willing to help all that he can.

Limitations

The limitation in counseling that most ministers acknowledge is the lack of specialized training, but there is a more basic limitation that they must overcome. Even before receiving advanced training in this area, the minister must adapt his attitudes and approaches in other areas of his ministry to encourage openness between himself and those in his congregation. When he prepares himself to counsel through reading, classwork, and experience, he is also preparing the congregation. William Hulme states that "this relation of the counseling program to the other areas of the ministry begins in the pulpit." He observes,

> If there is a no-two-sides-to-the-story attitude in his preaching, they may feel they know what he would say anyhow. If he sounds as unbendable as a stone wall, they may fear his judgment upon them. If he preaches as though genuine Christians did not have problems—doubts, lusts, anxieties, resentments—his people will feel so guilty in having them that they would be afraid to bring them to his attention. On the other hand, if his sermons show an understanding of human problems and an attitude of love, these people will feel that he may understand them and also help them.[6]

Often the secret of successful counseling is more in one's attitude than his ability. The minister needs to emphasize simple, human methods such as sitting and listening. This is a fundamental service, as old as man. His limitations in ability will be understood and overlooked if he comes across as one who is genuinely interested in the needs of the flock.

When we feel inadequate to give advice, we can always turn people to the Scriptures. While one may not agree with the direct methods that Jay Adams urges, surely all can appreciate his emphasis on "nouthetic" counseling—"a verbal counseling confrontation in which change in beliefs, attitudes and behavior is brought about by practical use of scriptures in order to honor God and bless the one who is confronted."[7] We can also be guided by the Biblical injunctions that apply to counselors.[8]

Limitations of time rapidly become evident. Some ministers are ready to throw up their hands and call all counseling a waste of time, having become burdened by hours upon hours of listening to people's problems with little of value to show for their efforts.

Limitations on time will depend on the kind of counseling being offered and the urgency of the counseling situation. Some individuals simply want attention and desire to monopolize the preacher's time. Others really want help. It is wise to talk with those who are troubled as soon as possible after they request it. Such initial visits may need to be brief, because of other commitments. Even a brief catharsis can provide some relief for the individual. Basic suggestions can be given. A later appointment can be set up. In the case of urgent needs, one's schedule may be rearranged to help meet the problem promptly.

Most counseling situations, however, are less urgent. They can be scheduled on a regular basis with definite time limitations. The minister might say, "I'd be happy to talk with you. I'll have forty-five minutes free on Thursday afternoon. Let's plan to get together at 2:30 at the church." In doing this, he has set a limitation before the meeting ever begins. He can then control it more effectively. As other workers (especially the elders) are trained to assist, the demands on the minister's time will be lessened.

How far should a minister go in "deeper-level" counseling? Wayne Oates defined the minister's limitation this way: "He should go as far as his training has equipped him to accept responsibility for the outcome of his treatment. He should go as far as the uncontrolled environment in which he works will permit him to accept responsibility for the person's life and, finally, he should go as far as the limitations of his time and social role will permit him to give himself to the needs of the individual."[9]

Development of a Program

1. *Beginning.* The best place to counsel is in the church office. The church office is conducive to a Scripture-centered discussion of problems. Various resources are at hand for sharing with the individual. The location saves the minister time in travel. It can serve as a protection for the minister (by having

the secretary present in the next room) when counseling a woman alone. Also, the termination of the interview can be handled more smoothly there.

The time allotted for counseling may vary with each location at which counseling is offered. While a minister might announce a general policy ("I plan to be in the office from 8:00 to 11:30 a.m. each morning for study, office work, and counseling"), it is difficult to set up regular hours to which counseling work can be confined. Frequently, the minister will need to make counseling hours available in the evenings, due to the work schedule of the people involved.

Careful records should be kept. The failure of some ministers to keep good records has been partly due to the confidential nature of the work, partly to a failure to understand the importance of records. Keeping adequate records is not only helpful to the person receiving the counseling, but it also helps the minister develop the discipline of a professional counselor. Varied records can be helpful—a detailed verbatim (full notes on an interview), a summary of the call, or a simple listing of the person and the date with no reference to the nature of the discussion. The careful minister will use all three types of records, for he will have people with varying degrees of need.

2. *Premarital counseling.* The minister is obligated to teach the meaning of marriage to all couples whom he chooses to unite in wedlock. He should discuss with them basic concerns such as the financial, social, sexual, and spiritual parts of marriage. (A fuller consideration of the material to cover in these interviews is offered in Chapter 20 under "Weddings.") In premarital counseling, the minister can train the elders to share in this pastoral work.

3. *Family Counseling.* While one normally thinks of marriage counseling as dealing with problems, the breadth of ministry to the home is much wider than that. Preventive as well as problem-solving counseling is needed. Training programs within the church can be designed to meet the needs of parents and children alike.

A significant portion of the minister's counseling will, however, be with those who are experiencing difficulties within marriage. Sociologists observe that most marriage problems stem from one of three areas—sex, money, or in-laws. You may quickly come to agree with their conclusion! Frequently the principal work of the minister is to induce communication.

When a husband and wife can talk things over—even if they disagree—the problem can frequently be worked out.

The minister must put all of the decisions in a Biblical perspective. He must remind each member of the family of the Scriptural injunctions that pertain to him (or her) as noted in Ephesians 5, 6 and elsewhere.

4. *Vocational Counseling*. While most vocational counseling seems concentrated in the guidance office of the high school, this also is an appropriate field for the minister. Indeed, if ministers would suggest more vigorously the available opportunities for specialized Christian service, many more young men and women might prepare for church-supported vocations. Whatever one's talents and interests may be, God can use them in some phase of specialized Christian service.

Job referrals, work-related problems, and other matters will also be included in the preacher's consideration.

5. *Crisis Counseling*. It is frequently at the time of tragedy—such as an illness, accident, or death—that the minister is called to help a troubled family. He must be sure of his theology! When people ask, "Why did God do this?" he can remind them of the distinction between what God causes and what He permits. He can describe how sin marred the perfect world in which God desired man to live (pictured in Eden). He needs to remind them of the hope that lies beyond this life for the Christian.[10]

It is frequently not so much what one says, but that one cares enough to come at such a time. Simply to be available as a compassionate listener is valuable. Many a minister has reached people for Christ by helping them through difficult situations. By seeing the love of Christ in action, they became willing to listen to the claims of Christ upon their lives.

6. *Training others*. The minister who learns to counsel will want to share his ability and experience with others. He will see the Biblical perspective, which makes the elders responsible for shepherding the flock. The elders can be especially helpful in premarital counseling and when the preacher must counsel with a single woman. If the minister offers and provides the training, some (but not all) will be willing to accept it. He may need to begin with just one elder who is willing to show that it can be done in order to persuade others to try it.

As the minister counsels, he must realize that he is a representative of his Lord. His desire is to help people find the love and understanding that Christ has for them. Wayne Oates singled out the difference of the Christian's role from that of the world in this way:

> The Christian pastor, therefore, cannot select his clientele; he cannot eliminate those whose plight does not come under the classification of his specialty; neither can he pass hopeless cases to someone else. Regardless of the other ministers to humanity who may be serving his people (whether those servants be doctors, nurses, lawyers, social workers, psychiatrists, welfare workers, or public-school teachers), the pastor, by virtue of his role as a man of God, can never consider his people as being some other person's responsibility to the exclusion of his own. He *cannot pass his ministry to anyone else.*[11]

Supplemental Readings

Jay E. Adams, Competent to Counsel. Baker, 1975.
Jay E. Adams, The Use of Scripture in Counseling. Presbyterian and Reformed, 1970.
William Hulme, How to Start Counseling. Abingdon, 1955.
David R. Mace, Success in Marriage. Abingdon, 1958.
Wayne E. Oates, Pastoral Care and Counseling in Grief and Separation. Fortress, 1976.
J. C. Wynn, Pastoral Ministry to Families. Westminster, 1957.

Related Projects

1. After familiarizing yourself with the basic counseling techniques, write a verbatim (a full set of notes) of an interview. Ask an experienced minister to assess your work and make suggestions.
2. Locate a Christian counselor or psychiatrist in your area to whom you might refer a member of your congregation. Ask other ministers in the area for suggestions.
3. Outline the steps that one should take to begin a counseling program in the local congregation.

---

[1]2 Timothy 4:2
[2]Kennedy, The Seven Worlds of the Minister, p. 90
[3]Adams, Pastoral Counseling, p. 16
[4]Ibid.
[5]Oates, The Christian Pastor, pp. 43, 44
[6]Hulme, How to Start Counseling, p. 13
[7]Adams, loc. cit.
[8]For example, Galatians 6:1 and Jude 22, 23

[9]Oates, *op. cit.*, p. 191

[10]See my article, "Knowing God's Will," in *Christian Standard*, February 14, 1971; and *The Will of God* by Leslie Weatherhead, Abingdon, 1944.

[11]Oates, *op. cit.*, p. 47

17

Administration

As you read, think about these questions:
—What are some of the Biblical precedents for administration as a part of the ministry?
—How can a minister help himself in his work by being a capable administrator?
—What are the limitations of the minister's work as an administrator?

"I like to preach—but I just can't stand administration." This is the complaint of many a modern minister. Others explain that, while they can do administrative work, they do not feel that it is important, much less essential.

Just what is "administration"? The dictionary tells us that it involves managing, directing, and handling executive duties. It is not shuffling papers, thinking up unimportant jobs for busy people to do, or keeping oneself tied behind a desk. Administration is simply good planning and organization.

A Biblical Basis

Jesus was an administrator. Note His pattern of ministry—Judea, Galilee, Perea, Samaria. Notice that when He fed the five thousand He had the multitude sit in groups of hundreds and fifties.[1] His work was orderly, His pace unhurried, His relation to others excellent. Throughout His ministry, our Lord neither practiced nor condoned slipshod, careless work. Always, in all circumstances, He was well prepared. He directed His followers in both short-term and long-range campaigns toward various objectives.

The apostles were administrators. They were aware of numbers as the church grew. When their work load became too great, they called for the selection of helpers who would minister in the church.[2] They attempted to involve people in leadership roles even of new congregations. From their days of travel with Jesus, they had learned the necessity of care and foresight in plans, attention to details, and concern for people.

Paul was an administrator. He used the printed page to cover vast reaches of land when he could not go personally. His missionary tours, his use of assistants, his training of other workers—all point out his administrative ability. He expresses the concept of training others for service in Ephesians 4:11-14. Throughout the New Testament wise planning and organization are evident in the church.

The minister's work has been described as the administration of the policies of the elders in harmony with the New Testament. He is responsible for stewardship of the talents of the people God has entrusted to his care. His efforts in management involve planning, leading, organizing, and evaluating. Such management is not a substitute for prayer, faith, revival, or anything else God has ordained for his work. Neither is it a synonym for leadership nor the result of a certain type of personality.

If one desires a Biblical basis for administration, let him turn to 1 Corinthians 14:40—"Everything should be done in a fitting and orderly way." This principle summarizes the minister's imperative for good administration.

A Necessary Function

Every minister knows the feeling of being torn between his various jobs. When he is studying, the preacher might feel he needs to be out calling. When visiting in a home, he might feel he should be working on a sermon. While it is difficult to find the balance, both activities are essential to a well-rounded ministry. If the people are to come, then he must go to them. But when they come, he must have something prepared to say.

One cannot be a great preacher without being involved in the total work of the ministry.

Good administration will let the minister minister. The minister's time must be organized to allow the proper amount for each of his many activities. He should be allowed eight to twelve hours per week to spend on sermon study. He needs time for counseling, office work, and special programs. The preacher should be able to make a number of calls each week—on the sick, on members, and on the unchurched. He should also have a day of rest.

Sounds good, doesn't it? This very concept of putting each role of the preacher in perspective requires administration. Priorities must be assigned to the most important tasks.

In his guide to management in Christian organizations, Kenneth Gangel notes that the word used in the New Testament to describe the gift of administration is *kubernetes*. This is a noun form that literally means "to steer a ship." Gangel notes the use of this term in Acts 27:11. The ship's administrator was the helmsman. He was responsible to note the "times of day; the nature and direction of storms; the habits of air current; the process of steering by the stars and sun; and because of his knowledge, to correctly direct the ship."[3] Just as the helmsman is the responsible decision-maker on the ship, so the minister may use the gift of administration[4] to help direct the affairs of the local church.

Unfortunately today the minister often seems caught in the cogs of an organizational machine. Some think that the church's mission has been hidden behind the vast amount of organization necessary to accomplish it. The following is an atrocious piece of doggerel that reflects this attitude:

> Like a corporation
> Works the Church of God;
> Brothers, we are treading
> Where Henry Ford has trod:
> We are all mass-minded,
> One huge body we,
> Planning world salvation
> Through the hierarchy.

Those of us in free churches have no denominational officers over us, but we still have plenty of organization to deal with! "Can't we do the Lord's work without all of this organization?" some ask. It depends on what one means by "all this organization."

A Crucial Task

For the minister, administration involves two main areas: (1) The minister will plan his own life and time; and (2) he will organize and implement the program that the elders have directed for the local church. His administrative work involves locating and training workers, replacing them when necessary, seeing that good communication exists among church leaders, sharing plans and goals with the congregation, and equipping others to do the work of ministry.

Every administrative circumstance has at least three components: the man, the work-group, and the situation. The preacher brings his personality and ability into his work. He is involved regularly with members of the congregation. The situation may include both the task to be done (organizational goals) and the organization required to accomplish it.

Administering the programs of the church is not always easy or pleasant. An old preacher heard a young man complain that he did not feel like preaching at certain times. The elderly gentleman advised him pointedly: "A good deal of the ministry, young man, is doing what you do not feel like doing, and doing it when it ought to be done."

The minister's work is not wholly administrative, but it cannot be done effectively apart from administration. Good administrative procedure calls first for setting goals. Next, planning and organizing are essential. The sign done by the clumsy printer brings a smile—"Plan Ahead." Planning involves looking ahead, anticipating and evaluating obstacles, and predicting outcomes. Liabilities and assets must be weighed. Then the organization and coordination of a program must be handled. One must check on each job that needs to be done:

1. Whose responsibility is it?
2. Is the person aware of his responsibility and prepared to carry it out? (If not, he needs information and/or training.)
3. Who will check to be sure it is completed (and to evaluate it, if need be)?

Brian Giese points out the need to link authority with responsibility.

One principle of good administration which is frequently overlooked is that a person should be permitted to administer the program for which he is held responsible. For instance, if a man is hired as youth minister, he should be allowed to formulate and administer the youth program of the church. The youth minister should be given a free hand to direct his own program without interference from the elders or the other minister(s), as long as he is fulfilling his responsibilities and is not violating any Scriptural teaching.[5]

Often the minister must find workers for various jobs. This work can be done through use of a Christian Service Interests sheet (see Chapter 21). The minister's goal should be to have every member of the church doing at least one job. Avoid overworking the few and overlooking the many. Let each person use his abilities where they are best suited.

The minister is not a dictator. He is not the board of directors, but the manager; he is not the commander-in-chief, but the general. He is a servant-leader who gives full time to do the work that the elders have approved.

The minister need not do all of the personal contact himself. He may need only to say a gentle word of reminder. On Thursday evening, for example, he might call the chairman of the mission committee. The conversation might go something like this:

> MINISTER: Hello, Don, I just wanted to check to see how the mission committee is coming on their plans for our Faith Promise Rally. At the board meeting next Monday I imagine we'll need to get started on the program.
> DON: That's right, preacher. I'm planning to get the committee together before then, but we haven't met yet.
> MINISTER: That's O.K. I just wanted to be sure everything was coming along. If you need any help from me, let me know.

If you phone back about five minutes later, you'll probably find his line busy. He'll be calling committee members to get that meeting set! All he needed was a little reminder.

Even in administration, the minister is not to do all of the work. Others can and should be involved at every step. In the plans for a new building, for example, a long-range planning committee may first begin the project. Another committee might select the architect. Others might help give input to the plans. Various committees can be formed for specific duties both during and after the building process. The dedication service itself would involve others. The minister could be involved in all of these to some degree. He should seek to present Biblical principles, encourage communication, and provide motivation.

Not every preacher has outstanding administrative ability, but every preacher must be involved in administrative work. One of the best definitions of administration is "getting things done through people." The minister is not to do it all, but he is to help others do it. He is to labor so that the work gets done—and is done well. Administrative work, while not usually thought of as "spiritual," helps the church accomplish the "spiritual" task that the Lord has assigned it. Through this ministry can be fulfilled the ideal: "For we are God's workmanship, created in Christ Jesus to do good works, which God prepared in advance for us to do."[6]

Supplemental Reading

Dayton & Engstrom, *The Art of Management for Christian Leaders.* Word, 1976.
Kenneth Gangel, *Competent to Lead.* Moody, 1974.
Olan Hendrix, *Management for the Christian Worker.* Quill, 1976.
Guy P. Leavitt, *Superintend With Success.* Standard, 1980 (revised).
Charles Livingstone, *Using the Sunday School to Reach People.* Convention Press.
Larry Richards, *Creative Bible Teaching.* Moody, 1971.

Related Projects

1. List all the steps involved in implementing the use of Christian Service Interests Sheets at the church where you serve. Place these steps in proper sequence. Set a target date by which you would have the initial program completed (at least three to four months from now). Then set preliminary deadlines (working backward from your target date) to help carry out the program. (See Chapter 21 for further information.)
2. Who should check to see that various jobs are being done? Discuss your church's present system with the elders. How can it be improved?
3. Write for a free subscription to the Christian Leadership Letter published by World Vision International, 919 W. Huntington Dr., Monrovia, CA 91016. Read and file the copies.
4. Share one of the readings suggested above with your Bible-school superintendent. After each of you has read it, plan an evening to discuss implementation of new ideas.

5. Talk personally with at least one teacher in each department of
your Bible school. Ask for suggestions on ways that you might
work with them. Be sure to get the names of new prospective members who may be attending their classes.

---

[1]Mark 6:40
[2]Acts 6
[3]Gangel, *Competent to Lead,* p. 19
[4]1 Corinthians 12:28
[5]Giese, "Church Administration: Whose Job Is It?" *Christian Standard,*
November 14, 1976, p. 11
[6]Ephesians 2:10

18

Motivation

As you read, think about these questions:
—What methods can a minister use to motivate others?
—Why is one's own attitude important in motivating others?
—What is leadership? What makes an effective leader?

Jesus tells us that a person's heart controls his destiny.[1] Thought has been called "action in rehearsal." Whatever one does is a result of the thoughts and motivations within him. The effective minister must be able to motivate others for service.

Your Attitude

An optimist has been defined as a person who, falling from the top of a forty-story building, says on the way down, "All right so far!" One does not have to be a Pollyanna to look on the bright side of life. Realism is necessary. But, for the Christian, God must figure prominently in reality! The current situation is never as bad as it seems. When Amos and Andy were on radio some years ago, Andy would describe *status quo* by saying, "That's Latin for the mess we's in!" The Christian will get in a mess occasionally. He will have problems. But he also has the assurance of God's Spirit to help him.

A person's success or failure is largely dependent on his own attitude and not on the circumstances under which he operates. A popular time-management teacher verified this idea when he said, "Nine-tenths of a salesman's success depends on management. One-tenth depends on his territory." Commenting on the statement, Mark A. Taylor, editor of *The Lookout*, said, "Circumstances don't measure our success. Maybe we don't have enough time, but we have as much as anybody else. Maybe our situation is difficult, but others have it hard too. What does matter is how we use our time. What is important is how we approach the circumstances we face."

It is all too easy to blame our failures on "the poor leadership at our church," or "the poor facilities we have," or "this little town where there's no chance to grow." Our biggest problem might be with ourselves, beginning with our attitude.

When you are working in the church, you are dealing with people. They are Christian people, to be sure—but still people. They get discouraged, have their feelings hurt, and get upset just as other people do. Just as you do, in fact. Realizing your own inadequacies will help you be sympathetic toward those of the congregation. If you are not too proud to admit your mistakes, the congregation usually will be big enough to forgive you. They'll also be more willing to admit their mistakes.

When someone complains to you, what do you do? Don't fear the complaint. Don't ignore it. Don't deny it. A problem has to be solved. Assume that it can be solved. Work with the complainer, making it easy for him to modify his claims and cooperate. If you have done wrong, be willing to admit it. In this spirit, you can show the true humility that makes one willing to learn from others.

A positive, constructive, optimistic spirit should characterize one's ministry. The preacher who always berates his people and harps about every failure cannot build a church. On the other hand, the minister who looks for the good and praises it, who recognizes potential for advance and encourages it, and who is quick to share the praise for good that is accomplished, is a minister who can motivate people.

Your Influence

The minister is to make disciples. This must start with his family, extend to church officers, and reach potential leaders for the future. A good minister works at reproducing himself in the lives of others. Paul said, "Follow my example, as I follow the example of Christ."[2] None of us lives as well as we should. We cannot ask others to do just what we do—we must encourage them to do what the Lord says to do. Still, we must model proper behavior for them as best we can. There is a world of difference between such a spirit of responsibility toward others and that of the pompous leader who brashly declares, "Do as I say, not as I do."

At the other extreme are those who say, "I don't speak of my faith; I simply let my life witness." How self-righteous can you get? Both the Word of God and the witness of life are necessary to teach and motivate others.

The Christian minister has the authority to motivate people toward the goals of the church, and with it comes the power to persuade—to influence opinion and induce belief. By using this authority, he can lead others to action. This authority should be exercised with the attitude of humble service.

The way in which we help others might be both surprising and refreshing. A minister told of a widow in his church who was lonesome and often depressed. He gave her the names of several shut-ins and asked her to help him keep in touch with them. She did. In the process she developed a friendship with several people she had not known before. She spent hours on the telephone with them. Each month she reported to the minister on how the shut-ins were doing or if they had special needs. "She was a different person," the minister said, when discussing the results of the arrangement. "By meeting the needs of others, her needs were met. That's exciting!"

The minister influences others by helping point them to Biblical goals for life service. The purest act of leadership has been described as setting a goal and getting others to accept it and work toward it. That is motivation!

Your Awareness

The successful leader is one who knows others and knows what motivates them. Management studies have listed these characteristics. Exceptional leaders

1. Have a high frustration tolerance.
2. Encourage participation by others.

3. Continually question themselves.
4. Are cleanly competitive.
5. Keep under control their "get even" impulses.
6. Win without exulting.
7. Lose without moping.
8. Recognize legal restrictions.
9. Are conscious of group loyalties.
10. Set realistic goals.

Such a leader is aware of life as it is and people as they are. He will plan, read, discuss, and arrange a strategy to accomplish his goals. Men in the secular world follow this procedure regularly. In this as in other ways, the children of this world are sometimes wiser than the children of light.[3]

One who would motivate others must get to know them. He must spend time with them. Regular business meetings are not enough. A minister's best friends should be his elders. He should be close to the chairman of the board, the Bible-school superintendent, and the mission chairman—not for the sake of "buttering them up" to ask for special favors, but to develop good communication so that worthwhile planning can be done. As the minister is aware of the needs and limitations of the people in the church that he serves, he will be better equipped to meet them.

The minister will build morale by helping each member realize the importance of his particular job. He will encourage confidence in the church leadership. Every contact he makes will be designed to encourage participation, so that church programs can become what "we" are doing, not "they."

Everyone needs recognition. Each Christian wants to be thought of as a person, not just a cog in the preacher's big machine. The expression of gratitude for a job well done, the encouragement of a congenial group relationship, and good communication are other ways in which your awareness can expedite church growth.

One of the finest testimonies to this spirit came from the late Dr. T. K. Smith. For thirty-five years, he ministered with the First Christian Church of Columbus, Indiana. In an address to the North American Christian Convention in 1965, he summed up his advice to preachers as "Love Thy People":

In the twenty-five years that I was secretary of the North American Christian Convention, whenever [P. H.] Welshimer was invited to speak, we made preparation quietly for someone to take his place if he were not able to attend the convention. He cared for his people so much that if one of his flock died or some of his members really needed him, he would not leave his church. Here you find one of the basic secrets of his success. He loved his people. . . .

Here is a challenge to every minister young or old. Would you succeed? Then love thy people. Love them so completely that nothing keeps you from a ministry of unrestricted service to them.[4]

The awareness of this kind of concern builds churches and motivates people.

Your Results

There are three dimensions to a leader's role in an organization, according to Dallas Meserve, and each one is necessary for organizational achievement: (1) The objectives of an organization tell a leader what to do; (2) proper organization helps the leader to do the job; (3) but the spirit of the organization determines whether the leader will be able to get the job done or not.

You may know all of the right answers, but if people won't ask the right questions or won't listen to what you say, your knowledge will do you no good. To succeed in the ministry, you must be able to work with people. If this area is difficult for you, consider some of the suggested supplemental readings.

As Moses learned from Jethro, it is impossible for one person to carry the whole load. Even if it were possible, it would be neither wise nor Scriptural. Each part of the body has a function. As an equipping minister, the preacher's role is to assist each part of the body to operate properly. With the right spirit, the motivation of each worker can be accomplished.

Supplemental Readings

Dale Carnegie, *How to Win Friends and Influence People.* Simon & Schuster, 1937.
Robert E. Coleman, *The Master Plan of Evangelism.* Revell, 1964.
Kenneth Gangel, *Competent to Lead.* Moody, 1974.

Related Projects

1. Read one of the books listed above. Outline in not more than two pages how you can implement the suggestions given in your present (or future) ministry.

2. Interview two of the most highly motivated people that you know. Ask them what suggestions they would give to help motivate others.

---

[1]Matthew 15:16-20
[2]1 Corinthians 11:1
[3]Luke 16:8
[4]*The Report* (The Cincinnati Bible Seminary), June, 1969, p. 3

19

Calling

As you read, think about these questions:
—Who should be called on? Where can prospects be found?
—What are some of the best ways for a minister to start a calling program at his church?
—In what cases is it best to make an appointment before a call?
—What are the advantages of bringing another person with you when you go calling?

An effective preacher once said, "The ringing of door bells is quite as essential as the announcing of texts." The preacher must call. The apostle Paul himself serves as an example at this point: "I have not hesitated to preach anything that would be helpful to you but have taught you publicly and from house to house. I have declared to both Jews and Greeks that they must turn to God in repentance and have faith in our Lord Jesus."[1]

The minister's work in calling will involve two areas—prospective members and members. Each category will be considered separately.

Types of Calls

Prospects

Literally an "evangelist" is one who carries the good news; he is a herald of God's provision for salvation. All who are not

Christians are prospects. Every person is one or the other—either a missionary or a mission field.

The minister has more training in the Scripture than the average church member and can give more of his time to the effort. Consequently he becomes more able in evangelism. It is essential that he never neglect the winning of souls. Even the minister who leads a large church with a staff of other paid full-time employees should recall that his work, like that of Jesus, is to preach the good news of the kingdom.

With the press of affairs, it is easy to neglect this part of his ministry. But such neglect can be fatal. Few souls are won simply by one's preaching from the pulpit, no matter how able an expositor of Scripture he is. The unsaved will not come regularly to church to be taught. The minister must go to them. He must bring them. He must enlist the aid of others in evangelizing them.

An equally important part of the preacher's work is to teach those who already believe to observe and obey their Lord's commandments. This teaching becomes especially crucial in the contacting and enlisting of those who should transfer their membership to the local assembly of believers. The inactive Christian also needs exhortation to be faithful until death.

One out of every five families in the United States moves during any given year. The involvement of these brethren in the life of the congregation where they relocate becomes important. Naturally one would hope that each member who moves to another area would feel the urgency of this step. In practice, however, most seem to need encouragement and direction. Here also the minister may assist.

With every other Christian in the congregation, he must seek to follow the example of the early Christians: "Day after day, in the temple courts and from house to house, they never stopped teaching and proclaiming the good news that Jesus is the Christ."[2]

Members

Some preachers believe that they are simply to preach the gospel to the unsaved and not be concerned about instructing Christians. This, they insist, is what an evangelist is to do. In contrast to this idea, Paul told Timothy to "point these things out to the brothers." In this way he would "be a good minister of Christ Jesus, brought up in the truths of the faith and of the good teaching that you have followed."[3] Certainly we may train elders to assist in the vital role of instructing Christians. Paul did not hold himself aloof from the work of the elders, but said to them, "In all things I have left you an example."[4]

Although the elders have the responsibility of shepherding the flock, the minister should also take an interest in the spiritual condition of the people as well. As he does his work in equipping the saints for the work of ministry, he will find many others who are pleased to share in this critical area.

When calling on members, a number of types of calls are necessary:

1. *Absentee.* Those who have not been attending the services need to be reminded of the Biblical admonition to assemble with the saints.[5]

2. *New member.* Occasionally a new Christian will say, "Before I was baptized, the people from the church called on me frequently. Since then no one has come to my home." The minister and an elder or deacon should personally visit every new member at least once following his conversion. The member should be taught in a special class. He will learn that it is then his responsibility to help reach others and not expect others to call continually on him (see Chapter 21).

3. *Sick.* Calls on the sick are crucial for the minister who wants to love and be loved by his people. Many see God best when they are forced to lie flat on their back and look up. Countless ministers have built churches through a strong, compassionate ministry with those who are ill. Never neglect to visit one who is sick when you are requested to do so, even if the individual has no affiliation with your congregation.

Perhaps the greatest mistake the minister can make when he calls on the sick is to stay too long. Brief visits are best. Rarely should he be seated in the sick room. Over fifty years ago, a minister gave this advice to young preachers: "One should be as deliberate in entering a sick room as if he were going to stay all day, but after a few minutes and certainly before the patient is weary (and the very sick weary very quickly), he should go."

It is never out of place to offer to have a word of prayer before departing. You might say, "I'll need to leave in a few minutes. Before I do, would it be all right if I had a word of prayer?" In almost every case, the request will be appreciated.

Even in the rare instance when an unbeliever does not wish you to offer a prayer, you will feel better for having attempted to minister to him. You will have also avoided offending him by asking his permission rather than going ahead to give prayer without asking.

When calling at a hospital, check with the nurse in charge before going to the room. You might ask, "Is it O.K. for me to visit with Mr. Jones for a few minutes? I'm his minister. I didn't want to disturb him in case he is resting." This is especially important when the minister goes at other than the normal visiting hours. Most hospitals will permit a minister to come at any reasonable time. Do not abuse this privilege.

If the door to a room is closed, always ask at the desk before going in. If no nurse is nearby, you may knock, start to open the door very slowly, and say, "This is the minister. Is it all right to come in now?" This prevents disturbing the patient at an embarrassing time.

Always acknowledge the other patients in the room. In some cases you may be introduced to them by the one on whom you are calling. Some will want you to include them in your prayer. At other times, you may simply smile and say a word of greeting. Be open and friendly to them. You might be able to minister to them also.

Every minister should be attentive to the visitation of the sick. Our Lord himself indicated that this would be considered in the Heavenly Father's judgment.[6]

The great preacher (and teacher of preachers), J. H. Jowett, experienced what all find in the ministry—as we help others, we are helped by them. Jowett tells of visiting a man who had cancer in the throat. Time after time he talked with him. Never did a word of complaint escape his lips. Finally his voice sank to a whisper and at last the power of speech ceased.

The first time Jowett saw him after he became dumb, the man took a slip of paper and wrote these words on it: "Bless the Lord, oh my soul, and forget not all His benefits."

Jowett said, "I don't know what help I brought to him, but I know he gave to me a vision of the higher range of human possibility and of the splendid triumph wrought by the power of the divine grace."

4. *Bereaved.* Those who mourn need to be comforted. See Chapter 20 about ministering to those who have lost a loved one.

5. *Counseling.* A large part of a minister's work includes giving guidance to those who have questions and problems. Counseling is considered more fully in Chapter 16.

6. *"Social calling."* Should the preacher spend time dropping by to visit informally with a member or prospect? He will not likely have time for such contacts if he is doing the rest of his work adequately. In some communities, however, it seems to be an inherent obligation for the minister to make an occasional call in the homes of members. While this can be done when the minister deems it essential, the congregation should be taught that the minister wants to be available for everyone at times of need—but that he will not have the time to visit as often as he might wish for purely social exchange.

A brief item in the church paper on "when to call your minister" might help to inform your congregation of your policies on social visiting. If a minister does engage in social visiting, he should be careful that it is spread fairly over the entire congregation and not limited to a few select families with whom he enjoys fellowship. Whenever you are invited to a home for a meal, you are free to accept—this is different from choosing arbitrarily which members you will spend time with, and opening yourself to an accusation of playing favorites.

7. *Other calls.* Special groups within the church must not be overlooked. The elderly and the very young have special needs and should be given consideration. Wise is the minister who is their friend. James reminds us that pure religion includes looking after orphans and widows.[7] Many congregations are becoming increasingly aware of the needs of exceptional children. Those who have a physical or mental handicap need special love and attention. With whom can we better demonstrate the compassion of the Savior whom we represent?

A Calling Program

The minister must schedule definite times for calling. It is possible to spend eight hours a day in study, administration, or other worthwhile duties. If you do not program a place for visitation, you will find it easy to neglect.

Rarely can effective calling be done in the morning—unless it is in late morning hospital visits. Consultations with members by appointment in the church office or at luncheon discussions are also possible. The afternoon and evening hours are much better for calling.

In many communities (even rural areas), it is becoming increasingly difficult to contact people at their homes during the afternoon. In many cases even the man who lives on a farm may have an outside job and/or his wife may work outside the home. Careful appointments with those on shift work will help.

Evenings provide the best calling time. Even a late evening call (for example, 9:00 or 9:30 p.m.) can be acceptable providing one has made an appointment. Otherwise calling should be chiefly confined from 6:30 to 9:00 p.m. in most areas.

Calling by appointment has many advantages. You are assured that the person will be home and will be expecting you. He might be better prepared to talk concerning spiritual things. An appointment might sometimes present a difficulty for a first visit with a non-Christian prospect. I have frequently found that it is best to stop by unannounced on these people for the first call. By a brief, positive, friendly visit, you may set the stage for further teaching, disarm their prejudice, and establish rapport. Other ministers feel that even on these initial calls, appointments are preferable.

Sources of Prospects

As a minister begins—particularly in a rural or small town area—he might wonder where prospects are to be found. "There just aren't any here. Everyone goes to church somewhere or we've already called on them," he may be told. This is rarely the case!

Start with those who attend Bible school but are not yet members. These should be your best prospects. At least once each year, ask each Bible-school teacher to give you the names of every student attending class who is not on the church membership roll. You will be amazed at the number of prospects now attending of whom you were unaware.

Next go to the members and ask them to suggest the names of friends and relatives whom they feel might be interested. They will also be able to work with you in attempting to reach these prospects.

New residents are also a good source. Some ministers advise their church members to stop whenever they see a moving van unloading. Give the people a friendly greeting and a leaflet inviting them to attend church there the next Sunday.

Every visitor is a potential prospect. Careful records and prompt cultivation of these individuals will result in souls being added to the kingdom.

The Cultivation Process

Prompt personal interest pays off. In some areas it works well to call on each visitor during the week following his first attendance at worship. He should receive at least a phone call or note expressing appreciation for his coming. I prefer to send an individually typed form letter to each prospect after his first visit. Enclose a copy of the weekly church paper with it. Keep a list of these visitors on sheets, a separate sheet for each letter of the alphabet. When the person comes a second time, you may either add him to the church paper mailing list and/or send a second (different) letter. In that letter, you can mention that you hope to stop by and visit with him personally in the near future.

Such a practice accomplishes several things:

1. It does not "rush" the person. Some feel threatened by having someone from the church call on them the next day after they have visited.

2. It demonstrates immediate and continuing interest.

3. It allows the minister more time to spend with the better prospects—those who have been coming more than just once. An exception would be any visitors who request the minister to call or indicate that they are considering membership on the roll call cards. Naturally the minister would call whenever and wherever he is invited.

Involving Others

While the minister will lead in the visitation program, he cannot possibly do it all—nor should he. When he calls, he can take others with him. He might hold training classes for callers. He should set up a calling program in the church at the first opportunity. Some churches prefer to have a year round visitation program. In these cases, the callers would go out every week on a certain night (Monday seems to be the most popular). While such a continuous program is commendable if it works in your church, frequently people become reluctant to participate in a program that has no stopping point. Only the faithful few are there week after week. Better success can often be achieved with a calling program in which people are asked to make two calls per week during a three-month period. That would conclude their commitment.

Then after a month or two off, one could introduce a six-week calling program. After a break, another effort could be instituted and so on. In between time, training classes can be used to prepare more callers. Several programs have proved popular in various churches. Some of these are listed at the end of the chapter.

Callers should be provided with an information form giving basic facts concerning the prospects (see sample in Appendix). Be sure to keep a copy of the form in the office in case the caller loses his. It is advisable to make out a new form before giving one to a caller if some discouraging remark has been written down by the previous caller. For example, one visitor might write: "Not interested. Poor prospect." The preacher might feel differently. Another caller might have much better results. You do not want him to be prejudiced by the other visitor's bad experience.

Callers need encouragement. One new visitor was quite shy, so the preacher told him, "You'll find it helpful if you spend a few moments talking to God before you make the call." When the callers came back to report, the timid one came directly to the preacher.

He said enthusiastically, "Thank you for what you said about prayer. I tried it when I went on my call—and it works."

"I'm glad to hear that," beamed the preacher. "Tell us what happened."

"Well, I prayed the people wouldn't be home, and they weren't!"

Most people want to call, but don't know how. A training program led by a visiting evangelist and/or the local minister can help. A sheet outlining "Techniques of Visitation," containing a summary of instructions to be given to callers, can be found in the Appendix.

Principles for Calling

1. *Be impartial.* Don't ignore any members as you call. Do not confine your visiting to any special income or social group. Naturally you will have special friends—you would be something less than human if you didn't—but officially take care to regard all people as equal and serve them equally.

2. *Avoid the appearance of evil.* It is not wise for a minister to call upon a woman alone in her home. If you are calling on a married woman, go when her husband will be there. If this is not possible, take someone with you. The elders can help in this way.

All of the minister's relationships with those of the opposite sex should be kept clearly above reproach. The young minister in particular should be careful to avoid a compromising situation or even the appearance of an immoral relationship. It is hard to improve on the advice that Paul gave Timothy. He was told to treat "older women as mothers, and younger women as sisters, with absolute purity."[8]

3. *Let the person talk.* Do not feel that you are responsible to provide a thirty-minute lecture on a subject of your own choosing when you make a call! Be sensitive to the needs and interests of the person you are visiting.

4. *Go as far as possible in your teaching.* One of my early problems in calling was the idea that I had to go entirely through the plan of salvation every time I called upon a prospect. I later learned that this idea was wrong. Jesus didn't push people further than they were willing to go; neither did the apostles. They would take a person where he was and go as far as possible with him.

A positive witness for Christ and careful instruction in His Word are basic. While you will want to be positive and encouraging, do not be pushy. Always leave the door open for future visits.

5. *Establish rapport.* Learn the person's name. Pick up the names of family members. You may wish to keep these on a card or in a notebook to refresh your mind with pertinent facts before you go in for a visit. In most calling, it is advisable to begin with casual conversation and then move within a few (no more than five or ten) minutes into the basic purpose of the call.

6. *Take someone with you.* Calling with another person is an excellent practice. Go with an elder, your wife, your child, someone that you are training as a caller, a deacon, a Bible-school teacher, or a youth sponsor. The advantages are many. All that is said and done during the call can be established with the word of two witnesses. The other person can help take care of children or pets while you are teaching. He can pray for you. He will be learning. He can assist in the discus-

sion. He might add a word of testimony and encouragement to what you say. You have the opportunity to get better acquainted with the individual as you are traveling from place to place.

7. *Keep good records.* It is helpful to keep a copy of the church membership directory in your automobile. On it you can mark down the dates when you called on each member. A careful record of mileage travel should also be kept.

As you call you can say with William Ogden,

> Thus I would go on missions of mercy,
> Following Christ from day unto day,
> Cheering the faint and raising the fallen,
> Pointing the lost to Jesus, the Way.

Supplemental Reading

Paul Benjamin, *How in the World?* Standard, 1973.

D. James Kennedy, *Evangelism Explosion.* Tyndale, 1970.

Carl J. Scherzer, *Ministering to the Physically Sick.* Prentice-Hall, 1963.

Related Projects

1. Talk to an experienced caller, minister, or evangelist to learn how he attempts to lead a man to Christ. Practice doing it. Find an opportunity to put the method into actual use.
2. Write out five ways in which one can change the conversation flow from social visiting to a spiritual purpose when talking to a prospect.
3. Ask an experienced minister in the area to let you go calling with him. Notice what he does—as well as what he doesn't do. Afterward, ask him questions.

---

[1]Acts 20:20, 21
[2]Acts 5:42
[3]1 Timothy 4:6
[4]Acts 20:35
[5]Hebrews 10:25
[6]Matthew 25
[7]James 1:27
[8]1 Timothy 5:2

20

Conducting Services

As you read, think about these questions:
—What ways *besides* his sermon are available for the minister to guide the worship service and make it more meaningful?
—What should the minister do when someone responds to the invitation without fully understanding what he is doing?
—For which parts of the wedding preparation and ceremony is the minister responsible?
—How should a minister handle the funeral service of someone who was not a Christian?

The Worship Service

John Henry Jowett pointed out the need for ministers to be in control of the worship service: "The weakness of the pulpit is too often this: we are prone to drift through a service when we ought to steer."[1] This is the problem in the worship service that affects most preachers. Here are some suggestions for maintaining control:

1. *Plan the service.* Plan the entire worship service well in advance. Most of the time we plan our sermons in advance, although perhaps not as far ahead as we should. That is one value of a church paper. If you announce your sermon topic in the church paper, you are under pressure to preach on it Sun-

day. Some years ago a Florida minister, E. Ray Jones, preached for a men's banquet. He was asked to speak on an assigned topic. That night he said, "I want you to know that I have never preached this sermon before—under this title." That might be the way, occasionally, that we manage to preach on our announced topic, but we do need to give more thought to the planning of our sermons and the entire worship service.

Keep a record of sermons, music, and people involved in each service. The dates on which specific sermons were preached can be kept in a card file. Projections of future sermons can be used to plan for future participants in the service, appropriate hymns, and suggested special music (to be given to the choir director).

Check up on yourself. Are you simply preaching topical sermons week after week on whatever you happen to be reading? Have you stopped to see if some basic doctrines are being overlooked? Do you often take the congregation through a book in the Bible? I admit a strong inclination to expository preaching. I like to take a Bible book and go through it a chapter a week in sermons. Whatever you choose to do, you need some sort of plan for your preaching. Your plan should cover at least three months ahead and probably a year in advance.

Not only should you record sermons, but also the people you have used in the services. Who gave the benediction last Sunday? Did you just call on him the week before? Is there someone who has not led in public prayer recently?

Keep a list of the songs you use. You would be amazed at how much your choice of songs can contribute to a worship service. Teach new hymns occasionally. As you plan the service, vary the order once in a while.

2. *Involve people in the service.* People can be involved in the worship service in many different ways. They can lead in prayer (invocation, benediction, congregational singing, Communion, and offering), greet, serve Communion, take the offering, give a meditation before the offering or Communion, lead the call to worship, serve in the nursery, provide special music, sing in the choir, accompany singing, usher, and work in children's church. Use as many different people as you can.

You will be amazed, if you check, how easy it is to use the same people over and over again. You probably have a few select people that you frequently ask for prayer. They are always there. They are always there early. It's easy to ask them. But what about the others?

You will never know quite how much it means to some of these people until you invite one to assist. Ask a different person to pray every Sunday. Line him up a week ahead of time, and list his name in the bulletin. I have seen a man who, after having had time for preparation, gave such a fine prayer that I could tell he had thought about it all week. He said what he really wanted to say. His prayer meant something to him, to his family, and to everyone who heard it!

How much better that was than for me to give the prayer—or even to call on him unexpectedly. When I went to my first congregation, I was a freshman in Bible college. On the Sunday of my "trial sermon," about twenty-five to thirty people were there. I only caught the names of two or three men before the service. One man had already given the Communion prayer. So at the benediction, I called on the only other man whose name I could remember. I called him by name and asked, "Would you have the closing prayer?" He looked up with horror on his face and said, "I'd rather not!" I later learned that he had never prayed in public.

That experience taught me a lesson. Don't call on a person unless you know he is willing to pray in public. Even though he has been attending services for some time, he still might not feel comfortable to lead in public prayer. Those who are reluctant can be encouraged and taught; frequently they will do it later (as this man did).

Are you training young people to take part in the worship service? Some churches have youth take the offering on Sunday night and assist in other ways. The youth of the church might occasionally lead in all phases of a service.

Get different people involved in the worship service. Why should a preacher get up and do everything himself? We may say we do not believe in a clergy/laity distinction; we may declare we do not believe in calling one man "reverend." But what do we do? Do we expect the man (whatever we call him) who is up in front to do it all? If a minister has the feeling that he must give all the prayers, something is wrong with him. And if he does not have such a hang-up, why doesn't he ask some of the other people to participate?

3. *Give attention to music.* Not only should you examine the text of a hymn to see if it is Scriptural, but also communicate with the song leader and accompanist about the arrangements for music. If you try to be cooperative with the music

director, he is likely to cooperate with you! Problems come when you have poor communication. You need to be in touch with musicians about both the length and selection of music in the song service.

4. *Handle the invitation carefully.* Have someone else ready to receive people who come forward. The person can be an elder, deacon, or other member. He would give each of those who respond a card to fill out (see sample in Appendix). This arrangement is important. The minister must be concerned with continuing the invitation and greeting others who come, but at the same time someone should sit down and talk with those who respond. Some don't really know why they are coming and what is involved.

If you have a clear, simple card to be filled out, this is the best way to start. Some churches keep a little box with a supply of pencils, pens, and cards on the front pew. The person responding is asked to fill out the card while the invitation continues. (This is another good reason not to close an invitation while people are responding.) Then, when the invitation is over, the minister does not have to ask them why they have come or if they have been baptized. The card has done that. The person's birthday is obtained also for church records.

What if a person comes forward and you know that no one has talked to him about becoming a Christian? Should you go ahead and baptize him, or wait and study with him? The minister may talk quietly to him after the invitation along these lines: "Are you coming today because you really want to become a Christian, and give your heart to the Lord? Do you want to go ahead and be baptized this morning just like the Bible teaches?" If he answers, "yes," then I would proceed to receive the confession of faith in Jesus as God's Son and baptize him.

If he didn't seem to understand, I would suggest that we talk more after the service and baptize him later. I might say to the congregation, "This one comes with the desire to do what Jesus wants. He had expressed the need to study more concerning just what the Scriptures teach and I will meet with him to do this after the service. I know that you will want to be praying for him as he seeks to follow in what the Lord has commanded." By what we say, we can help to make it as clear as possible when we extend the invitation.

I have never given an invitation for rededication. I have had people come forward to rededicate themselves, though, and have tried to handle the situation as best I could when they did. It might be fitting to mention that one can rededicate his life wherever he is, and that many do it frequently in private. There might be times, however, when an individual feels a special need to publicly acknowledge the wrong in his life and ask the prayers of others to help as he tries to live a more Christlike life.

Normally I don't include an invitation to "specialized service." If I did, such an invitation would be after a special message and in an appropriate setting. Such an invitation should be careful to delineate that while all Christians are to be "full-time Christians," some can give all of their time to the Lord by entering a church-supported vocation. When we issue this invitation, we are inviting the person to train in a Bible college and earn his living by some form of vocational Christian service. Such an invitation need not belittle those who do not make this choice—but it can emphasize the need for "laborers for the harvest."

5. *Make the Scripture reading important.* Probably the greatest weakness in a typical worship service is the lack of significance attached to the reading of the Word. Emphasize Bible reading. Announce the text clearly. List the passage in the bulletin so that people can find it in advance. (Not all can flip to it rapidly!) Mention the version from which you will read. Practice your reading before the service. Stress the importance of this part of the service to the others who read Scripture. Some churches have the congregation use pew Bibles to read the Scripture in unison, and indicate the page number to which people should turn.

6. *Let the Communion be meaningful.* Add a special dimension with thoughtful meditations. For example, you could list all the names by which Jesus is called in the Bible, and use one for each Sunday's Communion meditation. This series of meditations would take you through one year.

Explain to visitors the way in which the Lord's Supper is served at your church. At some churches members partake as they are served, while others partake in unison. At least include a line in your bulletin about the procedure, or explain it orally. Emphasize that the Lord's table is for all of His followers, not simply those from the local assembly.

7. *Make the offering significant.* An offering meditation (or stewardship minute) is helpful. One of the church officers

might give the meditation each week, to remind people of stewardship continually instead of depending on a once-a-year sermon on giving. Some prepare offering envelopes with a message on them that can be read aloud. Testimonies on tithing can be used.

Some prefer having the Lord's Supper and offering together, while the men are in front serving. Others like to have the Lord's Supper at the very end of the service. If you collect bulletins, you can see what other churches are doing.

8. *Prepare well for baptisms.* Secure members to be ready to accompany those to be baptized. They can show the candidate where to find clothing, towels, and any other necessities. Make baptism a beautiful part of the service. Line up someone else in advance to read Scripture, and have another to lead a song while preparations are made. Some bulletins regularly include a hymn of baptism.

9. *Don't overlook the roll call and announcements.* I am a real believer in the silent roll call card. It is best to take them up at another time than the offering. They can be passed to the aisle at some point in the service (see samples in Appendix). Be sure to ask members and visitors alike to fill out a card at each service "to give us a record of your attendance."

Avoid reading all of the announcements. Proper use of a bulletin should greatly reduce the need for oral comments. You may need to correct an item or add a special exhortation, but don't read all of the bulletin. Some prefer having the announcements at the beginning of the worship service, while others like to have them last. Some churches read the names of new visitors and have them stand at the end of the service. Wherever the announcements and welcome are given, they must not distract from the worship service.

10. *The building itself must be prepared.* Heating, cooling, lights, PA system, pew ropes, bulletins, hymnals, roll call cards, pencils, offering envelopes—all must be cared for. This preparation requires the participation of many people. The preacher should not have to take care of these matters.

11. *Train ushers.* To find volunteers for ushers and other jobs, use Christian Service Interest Sheets. Teach ushers on a Sunday night prior to the evening service (while youth meetings are going on). After one or two training sessions, you can immediately put these people to work. You'll find you have a whole new group of workers.

A greeter can take the place of an usher in a smaller congregation. He must realize that his job is not just to stand at the
door until the prelude starts and then go sit down. A greeter
should stay at the door until ten minutes or so after the service
begins. He can greet latecomers (who, much of the time, are
visitors), and make them feel welcome. A husband and wife
team is ideal.

12. *Consider various orders of worship.* As you see bulletins from other churches, you will find ideas you might want to
try. Make changes gradually, however, and don't make too
many too soon after coming to a church.

13. *Teach your people to worship.*[2] Carefully instruct each
person who is participating. Follow the plan unless it is essential to make a change. Be sure of what you are to do in any
special observance (such as a Boy Scout presentation of colors).

The Scriptural rule for worship is that everything should
be done in decency and in order. It is well to precede the
service with a moment of communion with God.

Baptism

The Prerequisites

1. *The candidate.* Acts 8 is rich in instruction concerning
baptism. When the Ethiopian asked Philip if he could be baptized, Philip stated: "If you believe with all your heart, you
may." The eunuch said, "I believe that Jesus Christ is the Son of
God."

Philip had used the Scripture and "told him the good news
about Jesus." In this process, the nobleman learned that our
Lord commanded baptism. As they came to some water he said,
"Look, here is water! Why shouldn't I be baptized?" When one
preaches Jesus, he is obliged to instruct men on all that the
Lord has asked of His disciples. Those who wish to follow Him
desire to be baptized.

The criterion that Philip used to determine the man's
readiness for baptism was his faith in Jesus Christ as the Son of
God. This is in harmony with Mark 16:16—"Whoever believes
and is baptized will be saved." In every conversion account in
the book of Acts, those who were baptized had first come to
believe. This fits with the command of the Master recorded in
Matthew 28:18-20. Jesus said: "Go . . . preach . . . baptize . . .
teach." One who hears the Word might come to believe it.[3]

Those who wish to follow Jesus obey Him. Then they can be taught more.

2. *The baptizer.* No Scriptural limitation is given as to who can or cannot administer baptism. Obviously the person should be a Christian. Frequently it will be the minister—but not always. In many congregations, a father might baptize his child; a friend might baptize the one he brought to the Lord. There is no Biblical requirement that an "ordained minister" participate.

3. *The water.* The Gospel records that John the Baptist did his immersing at Aenon near Salim, "because there was plenty of water."[4] When the eunuch saw water ahead, he asked to be baptized. Sufficient water was available for both Philip and the eunuch to go "down into the water" where the baptism took place.[5] To immerse a person, the water should normally be at least three feet deep. One could baptize in a stream not quite this deep. Occasionally one might baptize a hospital patient in a bathtub. In the baptistery, however, it is relatively simple to retain the proper amount of water.

The Preparation

1. *The Place.* The baptistery should be kept clean and attractive. The rooms adjoining it and steps leading to it must be carefully prepared so that no one will slip on a wet surface. The water should be at least slightly warm, but not hot.

A robe should be provided for each candidate. Weights may be placed in the lower hem of the robe. Some churches provide cloth slippers and bathing caps, for those who need them. A good supply of towels is essential, as is a private place for the candidate to change clothes.

If the baptistery has drapes in front of it, they should remain closed until the candidate is in the water and ready to be immersed. When the candidate has come out of the water, the curtains may be drawn as he or she leaves the baptistery.

If one is baptizing in a river, make sure the candidate faces downstream. Check the river bottom thoroughly before going out, to be sure that there are no sudden drops. Have someone standing by with a robe or blanket to place around the candidate after the baptism.

2. *Assistants.* It is helpful to have at least two people available to assist in every baptism. A woman and a man in the congregation can be given this duty. They would assist those of

their own sex by showing them the baptismal garments and answering questions. One of them might also assist with the lights or drapes. The minister should use baptismal boots so that he can remain dry (fisherman's waders are satisfactory). In this case an assistant can help by hanging these up and by wringing out towels, so that the minister can go out to greet other brethren while the candidate is drying off and dressing. These assistants should be prepared at every service to come forward immediately after an individual has made his confession of faith to accompany him to prepare for the baptism.

3. *Instructing the candidate.* The candidate should understand what baptism means. You should explain the significance of the symbolic death, burial, and resurrection taking place in the water. Use Romans 6:3-8. The seriousness of the occasion should be stressed—especially to young people. You may wish to suggest that they look straight ahead, not at the congregation.

The physical act of baptism should also be carefully explained. You may wish to show the person in advance how he is to hold his hands, what you will say, and what he is to do. Normally I ask the candidate to hold his right wrist with his left hand. A person might wish to hold his nose; others want a handkerchief over it. I place my left hand over his hands and my right hand under his shoulders, after having given the baptismal formula. The candidate should be instructed to bend back easily at his knees and be lowered gently. Assure him that you will bring him right up. Allow time for the candidate to ask any questions. You may wish to quietly repeat this instruction in the baptistery as you prepare to do it.

A very large candidate might kneel in the water and the minister would place his hands on his head and gently push it forward to baptize him. It is sometimes necessary to baptize an invalid sitting in a chair. This person may be baptized in the same way.

Do not rush the baptism. Arrange for it to be a beautiful, meaningful part of the worship service.

The Service Itself

After the candidate makes his confession of faith in Jesus, he may be seated on the front pew of the auditorium. The minister may receive the confession of any others who have come forward. He should then instruct the congregation that a song and/or Scripture will follow while preparations are made for the baptism. Then, turning to the candidate, he can quietly say, "Would you go to that door to prepare for the baptism?" One of the assistants can accompany the individual.

Arrangements should be made before every service for those who will handle the pre-baptismal part of the worship. An appropriate hymn may be sung. One of the elders might read Scripture. The hymn and Scripture reading emphasizes the meaning of baptism to the congregation, and allows time for the candidate and minister to be prepared for the baptism. It is effective to have the sanctuary darkened with the only light centered on the pool.

The minister should step into the baptistery first. Assist the candidates as they come in or go out. Take your time. After the baptism, you may want to say, "God bless you," or "That was fine."

After the last baptism, the minister should either dismiss the service from the baptistery or arrange for someone in the congregation to handle the closing. Arrange to have Communion served to the candidate as soon as he or she is dressed. Friends will want to greet the person then.

The baptismal formula varies among individuals. One might say something like this: "Because of your faith in Jesus Christ, I now baptize you into the name of the Father, the Son, and the Holy Spirit, for the forgiveness of your sins." This statement incorporates the wording of Matthew 28:19, which should always be used. It also suggests one of the other aspects of baptism—the forgiveness of sin, as taught in Acts 2:38.

Other Scripture passages about baptism can be incorporated with the statement. For example, 1 Peter 3:21 (King James Version) suggests, "You are now baptized for the answer of a good conscience to God through the resurrection of Jesus Christ." Galatians 3:27 also explains further about the act that is taking place: "All of you who were united with Christ in baptism have been clothed with Christ."

Weddings

Whom will you marry?

Several theological questions must be dealt with by the minister who plans to perform a wedding. Will you marry only those who are members of your local congregation? Will you marry a couple if one of them is divorced? What if the divorce occurred before the individual became a Christian? Would it make a difference if the divorced person were the "innocent party" and the former partner had been unfaithful?

These are hard questions—and the answers are not getting any easier. With the frequency of divorce, the ease of remarriage, and the pressure of a society that largely forgets God, the minister will be hard pressed to find a completely satisfying and consistent policy. Whatever your determination is, let me urge you to base it on Scripture. Be firm and fair in following it. Most people will respect you, if you choose not to perform a marriage because of reasons of Scripture and/or conscience, unless they later find that you married another couple in a similar circumstance.

What conditions will you set?

An increasing number of ministers insist on having a minimum number of premarital conferences with any couple that they marry. Such sessions will include teaching (or giving the couple access to teaching) on all of the vital facets of married life. Such subjects as the financial, social, sexual, spiritual, and personal parts of marriage should be discussed. The ceremony itself can be planned. It is helpful to have a form prepared that the minister can fill out during the initial interview.

I have found it helpful to give couples material to read between conferences. I especially like the two books by Charlie Shedd—*Letters to Karen* and *Letters to Philip*. These books were written for two of his children and give practical advice not frequently touched on in other more familiar resources. Paperback copies make this an inexpensive gift. Filmstrips can also be used along with recordings and other teaching aids. Teaching can either be private or in group classes, if a number of engaged couples are being counseled at a given time.

What preparation should you make?

A wedding checklist should be given to the couple at the first session (sample included in the Appendix). This lists most of the items on which the bride or groom need to check. If the church does not have a stated policy on wedding arrangements, one should be drawn up at a board meeting. It is then given to each couple planning to be married there. A number of good books on wedding etiquette are available for reference.

Occasionally the minister will be asked by a couple, "What do you charge for the wedding?" You will have to decide how to answer. Some preachers feel that since the church wedding is optional, those who choose to have the more elaborate ceremony should pay for it. These brethren do not object to setting a fee. While I respect their right to do this, I have never done so. If pressed, I might say, "For a wedding like this I usually receive around $_____—$_____, but I don't have any set charge. Whatever you wish to give will be fine." This would suggest a range, but would also make it clear that you are not setting a fee. Traditionally the money received from weddings is given to the minister's wife.

The rehearsal date should be set as far in advance as possible. As soon as the couple request it, it should be checked on the church calendar. This emphasizes again the need for one central calendar on which to list every church event. Both rehearsal and wedding time should be entered.

It is the responsibility of the couple to notify all of the participants involved. Don't let yourself get the task of trying to arrange for an organist, soloist, and custodian. You can provide suggested names—but let the couple contact them.

Stress that the rehearsal will begin on time and that it will not be lengthy. Spend the opening minutes getting acquainted with each member of the wedding party. Be sure to ask only the bride and groom your questions pertaining to the wedding ceremony. Occasionally friends or relatives will attempt to answer for them and let their wishes become the rule. Refuse to let that happen. If someone gives a suggestion on what to do, politely ask the bride, "And how do you think it would look best?" Then follow her preference.

Begin with every person standing at the front just as they will in the ceremony. After they are all in place, go through the mechanics of the ceremony. Then have them go out as they will in the recessional. Next practice coming in. Then do everything once more. The second run-through—both going out and coming in—is to be certain that everyone understands. Then ask, "Does anyone have any questions?" If not, remind them to be at the church at least one hour prior to the time for a formal wedding, or one-half hour early for an informal one.

The minister can make quiet suggestions to assist, ask questions on matters that don't seem clear, and reassure all involved!

Some things to check on:

1. Instruct the ushers on how to seat the people. Explain about excusing the congregation row by row at the close of the service. Be sure that they know who is to escort the mothers in and out and at what time.

2. Be sure that the rear door of the auditorium is closed by an usher until the processional is over. Latecomers can then find seats.

3. See that the one giving the bride away knows what to say. When asked, "Who gives the bride away?" instead of answering, "I do," some fathers prefer to say, "Her mother and I." Remind him to be seated next to his wife immediately after he responds. He should step out into the aisle and allow her to take the usher's arm when they are escorted out.

4. Be sure that the wedding party understands where they are to go for the receiving line. If they plan to stand outside, help them choose an alternate place to use in case of bad weather.

5. Go over any special parts of the service—such as the lighting of candles, or kneeling—with those involved. Remind the bride to be especially careful going up and down stairs with her long dress.

6. Instruct the maid of honor about when she is to receive the bride's bouquet during the ceremony. Tell her when it is to be handed back. Suggest other assistance she might give—such as in smoothing the veil.

7. Ask those who hold the rings to put the ring on the index finger for passing from one person to another. It can then be held securely by the thumb and middle finger to avoid dropping it. When the bride and groom each give the rings to the other, tell them to slide it on only so far as it will go easily. Let the person receiving it work it past that last knuckle!

8. Remind the couple to bring the license to you before the wedding. Fill it out after the wedding, while the pictures are being taken or while guests are being greeted. The best man and maid of honor should sign as witnesses. You may give the license directly to the groom as you wish them well before leaving. The certificate may be given to the best man if this is more convenient.

9. Be certain to keep records of all marriages that you perform. Before performing a marriage, learn the legal regulations of the county in which it is being performed and abide by them.

What of the wedding itself?

Most minister's manuals include a wedding service. Many wedding services are available in booklet form, so that the minister can give the bride and groom a copy of the actual ceremony that was used for them. I particularly appreciate the service adapted by Edwin Hayden from one that P. H. Welshimer used (see Appendix). This simple service does not include the words for those who desire to repeat the vows, however. These can easily be obtained from other sources. Occasionally individuals wish to write part or all of their wedding ceremony including the vows. I have tried to cooperate with these efforts, as long as they were in harmony with Scripture. I always reserve the right to add some appropriate Scripture to these ceremonies.

In one of the early interviews with the couple, the minister should ask if they wish to repeat the vows or just say, "I do." If they wish to repeat them (and especially if they wish to memorize them), they should start early to get familiar with them. The minister should have a copy before him during the service, to prompt those who may become nervous and forget.

The wedding service is better when the minister has the ceremony memorized. You should at least be so familiar with it that your delivery is completely natural and sincere. Don't give the impression that you are reading it. Your reassuring word and smile can help a nervous couple. Indicate to them when they are to hand you the ring or join hands, by words in the ceremony, if possible. Use a simple nod or motion, if the instruction is not included in what you say.

If the couple plans to kneel during the song and/or prayer, suggest that they practice kneeling at home without moving for about seven minutes, so that they will be aware of the time and difficulty involved. Be certain of the way in which the couple want to have their names given in the service. Be sure that you can pronounce them properly.

Photographers, if allowed, should not be conspicuous at any time and must not intrude upon the service. Time for taking pictures can be allowed after the service. You can offer to pose for any pictures then. Some photographers take pictures during the ceremony without using flash and by not moving about a great deal. In such cases, disturbance is avoided.

After the service is complete, you may invite the groom to kiss the bride. He will lift her veil with both hands and put it back over her head. The maid of honor may help straighten it. After she has received her bouquet back from the maid of honor, have the couple turn and introduce them to the congregation: "It is my joy to present to you Mr. and Mrs. _____ _____." Occasionally they will want you to say a word of welcome and invite everyone to the reception. Normally this message would have been handled through the invitation, however.

Funerals

At no time may the minister be more of a minister to his people than at the time of death. The needs of a bereaved family should take priority over almost every other concern. On learning of the death of a church member, regular attendant, or relative of a member, the minister should call as soon as possible upon the family.

Frequently one will first learn of the death in the congregation from the funeral director. Remember as you talk to him by phone that it is quite likely that the family is seated in the room with him. Phrase your questions accordingly. In the case of a suicide, the funeral director will usually let you know privately. He will provide you (prior to the service) a brief obituary about the individual. These should be filed for future reference.

You should take care not to appear to be "asking" for the privilege of conducting the person's funeral. Normally the family is expecting and wanting you to do it, if the deceased is a member of the congregation. Even then, there will be times when a special request will have been made by the individual that a former minister or other preacher friend conduct or take part in the service. Do not be offended by this. Simply seek to minister to every family as best as you can, in the spirit of Christ.

Don't feel that you have to have "all the answers" to questions that may be raised by a grieving family. Your love, kindness, and concern is indicative to them that you care and want to help. When they ask, "Why did God let this happen?" or "Do you think my unbaptized mother went to Heaven?" or "What am I going to do now that I'm left alone?" or a hundred other questions, it is frequently best to say quietly and simply, "I'm not sure that I can answer that. But I do want you to know that I'll help in any way that I can. Remember that God still cares about you. He'll be here to help you also."

On more times than I can remember, I have driven to a home from which death has snatched one in an especially tragic circumstance. I have wondered, "What will I say? How will I start talking? What can I do to help them?" On each occasion, I have committed the situation to the Lord and resolved that I would share in a Christlike way any words of Scripture or personal encouragement I could. I have never found the Lord to leave me alone in these difficult situations. He will bless our efforts. Though the people may not remember all we say, they will remember that we cared enough to come.

Frequently it is best to give a simple word of condolence upon arrival such as, "I was so sorry to hear about your father's death" or "We were so shocked to learn that your boy was killed." The family frequently needs to talk. They need someone to listen. An occasional question such as "How did it happen?" or "Had he been sick long?" or "How old a person was your mother?" may be enough to help them begin. As they talk you can encourage them quietly, answering questions where possible, and reassuring them of God's care.

Before leaving the home, be sure to receive at least the basic information that you will need concerning the funeral (if the family has had time to make these plans). Will it be at the funeral home, the church, or elsewhere? Will others be participating—such as a lodge, or military personnel? Where will the burial be? Do they have special requests concerning Scripture or music?

Frequently the family will hesitate about selecting a specific Scripture passage. I normally say, "Would you just like me to choose something appropriate?" They will usually agree. Occasionally they will later find a special verse or a poem in the Bible of the deceased that they might ask you to include in the funeral message. It is good to use these, wherever they are fitting and can be worked in.

In going over service plans with the family, a member will sometimes say, "Just keep the service short." You can assure the individual that you will simply read appropriate Scripture and offer brief remarks. Many individuals are fearful that a preacher will use the funeral as an opportunity to berate them for their shortcomings. He shouldn't. The funeral service can provide an opportunity to minister to and later evangelize others in the family—but the funeral itself is not a revival meeting.

After everything has been discussed, you might say, "Would it be all right for me to read a word of Scripture and have prayer before I leave?" I have never known a person (church member or not) to refuse such an offer at this time. Psalm 121 is especially helpful. Psalm 23, of course, is good. You will find other suggested passages in various funeral manuals. After prayer, you might want to visit a moment longer, particularly if the family continues to be distraught. Then graciously take your leave with the assurance, "Let me know if you need anything. I'll plan to see you at the funeral home during the visitation time."

In the time that follows, you will want to be certain that others in the church are notified, including these people:

1. Ladies who might prepare food for the family on the day of the funeral.

2. Those who order flowers for the church to send to the funeral.

3. The custodian (if the services are to be held at the church).

4. The person's Bible-school class, special friends of the deceased, and whoever edits the church paper.

In preparing a funeral message, it is frequently helpful to check back over the member's associations and participation in the church. Some meaningful sidelight that can be included in the message will frequently turn up—in a church paper, in talking with other members who knew the person, or in your own remembrance of the individual's work for the Lord.

Most ministers have several basic funeral messages that they use, with adaptations, for most funerals. My own practice has been to keep each funeral sermon in a separate folder. On the outside of it, I record the funerals at which it was used and the dates. Since (throughout most of the nation) funeral services in our society do not draw many outside the immediate family, one might use the same basic funeral message for several services as long as they involve different church families. There will be certain occasions when you will want to prepare a special sermon in view of the person and/or the circumstances of death.

The service for a non-Christian presents one of the most difficult challenges for the preacher. He must remember that he is not there to judge the person. He is to speak to the living. He is to speak where the Bible speaks. One of my favorite outlines (not original with me) is "Things That Abide," based on 1 Corinthians 13:13. I normally use it for the service of a non-Christian.

The outline begins by mentioning that the death of a loved one calls our attention to the transient, temporary nature of many things of this life. "Change and decay in all around I see/O Thou who changest not, abide with me." Some things do abide. Three are found in the text: faith, hope, love.

Our *faith* in God abides. Psalm 46 declares that our faith in God remains no matter what happens. We trust that God still loves us even when we lose someone who is dear.

Hope abides also. We have hope that there will be a day of resurrection for all men. You may specify the Christian's hope based on various New Testament passages without stating whether or not these apply to the deceased.

Love also abides. At this point, I like to mention something good about the person that will be remembered by family and friends. Our love for another person does not end with death. More than this, God's love abides. He will continue to care for us and sustain us. Romans 8 is helpful. Such a message points men to God and His Word and draws attention to the good that a person has done, yet does not hold out false hopes.

Plan to go to the funeral home at the time of visitation. Say a brief word to the family, get any last instructions from them, and go over the arrangements with the funeral director.

Arrive at least ten minutes ahead of the scheduled funeral time. The minister should dress in a dark suit, tie, and shoes. The service should be brief. Twenty to twenty-five minutes is long enough, except in unusual circumstances (when the funeral is handled as an entire church service).

The service would include music (if desired), Scripture, prayer, sermon, and closing prayer. Vocal music can be interspersed throughout the service or used before and after the minister speaks.

When the service is over, the minister stands at the head of the casket while those who wish to do so file past the casket. When the immediate family of the deceased comes afterward, he may stand near the casket with the family. Warmth and sympathy are imperative; he should avoid a professional attitude. After the family leaves and the casket is prepared, the minister walks ahead of it to the hearse and, at the cemetery, precedes it to the grave.

Stand at the head of the grave. When the funeral director indicates that all is ready, begin the brief committal service. Normally only a passage or two of Scripture and a closing prayer are required. My preference is always to make Psalm 23 the last Scripture read. I know of no more fitting committal passage. Sample committal prayers are available in the various minister's manuals. Use their ideas, but not their exact words.

The funeral director will normally say a word to the people after the service. When he has done this, you may step up to the family. Say a quiet word of assurance such as, "I want you to know that I will be praying for you." Do not stand around as though you are waiting to be paid. After you have spoken to the family, feel free to make your way *slowly* out of the group near the grave, visiting with others as you go, and leave when necessary.

In most cities today, the funeral director will give the minister a check as payment for his services. It should be understood that the minister neither expects nor asks for a fee. If a gift is offered, it need not be refused. Some ministers use these gifts for some special fund in the church—or to purchase a book, in which the name of the family would be recorded as the donor. Visit the family again within the next few days. It is helpful to take with you a leaflet (such as that provided by the American Bible Society) that suggests Scriptures that would be helpful for the bereaved family to read.

The preacher may encourage a "funeral committee" in the local church. Such a group can assist with the details of preparing food, seeing that the building is prepared, and in other ways. The minister should also preach and teach about death.[6]

Much current literature addresses the preparation for death and the possibilities of life after death. Increasingly it is essential that parents explain to their children about death. Children should go to the visitation for someone who is not a close friend, so that they will have the experience without the added trauma of grief at the loss of a loved one.

Many funeral directors will provide free literature that explains about funeral services, costs, and prearrangement plans. Various state and national funeral directors' associations offer such literature for distribution.

The importance of allowing the family to express grief

cannot be overemphasized. Grief is a healthy emotion. The one who "keeps a stiff upper lip" may be in danger of an emotional problem later.

Many prefer to have the casket closed prior to the service so that it may end with a more positive, spiritual note. In some areas, a memorial service is held a few days (or more) after death, following a private burial. Such a service might be held in the church and be open to others.

Encourage the family to attend church on the next possible Sunday. The grieving widow may feel that it is hard to do so, but coming to church alone will not become easier by delay. Perhaps a good friend could be encouraged to offer transportation at that time. A brief mention of the death should be included in the announcements.

Supplemental Readings

Worship:

E. M. Bounds, *Preacher and Prayer.* Zondervan.

Lowell Russell Ditzen, *The Minister's Desk Book.* Parker, 1968 (Chs. 5, 8).

John Henry Jowett, *The Preacher: His Life and Work.* Harper & Bros., 1912 (Ch. 5).

William H. Leach, *Handbook of Church Management.* Prentice-Hall, 1958 (Chs. 14, 15).

William Robinson, *The Administration of the Lord's Supper.* Berean, 1959.

Baptism:

C. M. Perry, *Pastoral Problems and Procedures.* Baker, 1974 (pp. 154ff).

Weddings:

"Church Weddings Are Not for Everyone," *Christianity Today,* August 27, 1976.

R. David Roberts, "Responsibility for Weddings," *Christian Standard,* June 5, 1977, pp. 7, 8.

Funerals:

James L. Christensen, *The Complete Funeral Manual.* Revell, 1967.

Elizabeth Kubler-Ross, *On Death and Dying.* Macmillan, 1969.

Standard Manual for Funeral Occasions, Standard, 1953.

Herbert H. Wernecke, *When Loved Ones Are Called Home.* Baker, 1954.

Related Projects

1. Collect the bulletins from ten different churches. Notice the variety of arrangements in the morning worship service. What ideas and improvements for the worship service at your church can you find from these samples?
2. Attend either a wedding or funeral at another church. Notice the minister's role. Ask him privately for his suggestions to help you in a similar situation.
3. If you have not baptized a person, find a minister friend who will let you "practice" on him. Ask him for advice.
4. Talk with a local funeral director. Ask for the literature he has available. Some urban areas have a service center where one may view caskets just as the family would at the time of a loved one's death. Visit such a center, if possible.

---

[1]Jowett, *The Preacher: His Life and Work,* p. 148

[2]See also Lee Carter Maynard, "Meetin' House Etiquette," *Christian Standard,* August 22, 1976; W. R. Walker, "The Influence of Worship on Character," *Christian Standard,* 52 (1917), pp. 167, 168; and John Killinger, "How to Enrich Your Worship" (four cassettes from Abingdon Audio-Graphics)

[3]Romans 10:14-17

[4]John 3:23

[5]Acts 8:38

[6]For a suggested message, see my article, "If I Should Die," *Christian Standard,* October 23, 1965, pp. 9, 10

21

Implementing
the Program

As you read, think about these questions:
—What are the advantages of a committee system in implementing the programs of the elders?
—How can new members be quickly put to work in jobs suitable to them?
—What records should the church be keeping? What personal records should the minister be keeping?

The Bible clearly teaches that Jesus is the head of the church. Every teaching and every program is subject to His absolute authority. The specific plans carried out by a local congregation must be subservient to His will as revealed in Scripture.

Our Lord has entrusted each local congregation to the guidance of elders.[1] As they design and direct the program of the local congregation, the minister should assist in its administration. In some congregations where the elders have not been properly prepared (or where they lack leadership ability), it may be necessary for the preacher to assume a stronger role in suggesting and instituting such plans. Even in these cases, however, he must remember that he is not a "one-man authority" on church government.

For churches that maintain a congregational form of government (each congregation locally autonomous), church program arrangements are both simplified and made more difficult. On one hand, the minister need not be in touch constantly with a denominational authority who will tell him what that church should or should not do. Unworkable bureaucratic programs are avoided. On the other hand, it is easy to become lopsided and provincial without the balance of new ideas that consider a broader perspective. An even more sinister danger lies in the failure to plan adequately for long-range goals.

The Committee System

The work of the church should be classified and grouped under broad categories. An example of such an arrangement is shown below. Each category may be under the direct supervision of one or more elders. In a larger congregation, there might be two or more elders over each of the six categories. In a smaller church (or one that has only three or four elders), each elder might take one category himself, the total eldership might take another (such as worship), while the deacons might be assigned one section (such as fellowship and service). The advantages of the suggested committee breakdown are:

1. It keeps all programs under the supervision of the elders. When a question or problem arises in any phase of the church program, the elder in charge can be made aware of it and can lead in solving the problem. Matters that need to be referred to the elders as a group can be brought in by one of the elders. He will be closely involved in the activity and can report accurately on it.

2. Any size church can function under a committee system. The brand new congregation that starts with twenty or thirty members will immediately be made aware of the various matters to be considered as the church grows. Even before elders are selected by the congregation, the church may assign specific duties in the various areas to capable members.

3. The arrangement can expand with the church. A congregation may begin by using only the basic committees (the ones in capital letters on the list). All of the subpoints would then be included under the jurisdiction of that committee chairman. (That one person should not attempt to do all of the jobs himself.) Then as the church grows, the other committees can be added as needed.

Possible Church Committees

CHRISTIAN EDUCATION

Bible school
Children's church
Youth
Nursery
Vacation Bible school
Wednesday evening classes
Library
Teacher training classes

WORSHIP

Baptism
Hospitality
Greeters
Ushers
Communion
Auditorium
Flowers
Music

FELLOWSHIP AND SERVICE

Fellowship dinners
Athletics
Servicemen contacts
Public relations
Meals for sick or bereaved

STEWARDSHIP

Benevolence
Memorial
Finance
Counters for offering

PROPERTY

Church building
Grounds
Bus
Parking lot
Parsonage

EVANGELISM
AND NURTURE

Membership
Missions
Home department
Revival
Calling
New members

4. Finally in a large congregation (500 or more members), all of these committees (and perhaps others) can be included. You will see the importance of staffing the committee with different people to insure that the work is handled properly and that no one or two members are overworked.

Committee appointments should be made according to a general policy such as this:

1. The chairman of each committee is appointed by the chairman of the elders and/or chairman of the board.

2. Members of each committee are appointed by the elders' chairman and/or the committee chairman.

3. The elder who supervises each area is a member ex-*officio* of each committee in his area.

4. The minister is a member ex-*officio* of each committee.

5. All committee assignments are for one year only, unless otherwise specified.

Each committee is a group with a specific job to do. Temporary committees are formed to meet special needs. Normally committee members should be appointed on the basis of their interest in and fitness for the task the committee is to perform.

The committee chairman is the key person. He must be businesslike but congenial. His principal duty is to keep the discussion on the track. Frequently he can help the group arrive at a consensus. He should appoint a secretary at the outset of a meeting. The written report of the committee can then be circulated to the larger group to which the committee answers.

Not only is it Scripturally desirable to put every member to work, it is also pragmatically beneficial. Church members who are not involved in the program will soon lose interest and will fail to remain faithful to their commitment. The saying, "Use them or lose them," expresses the alternatives well.

When a new member comes into the congregation, he or she should be given a Christian Service Interest Sheet (sample in Appendix). The person's interests should be recorded and he (she) promptly should be assigned some role of service—or invited to some phase of training for service. Care must be given to match the people with the jobs and opportunities, especially in the case of assigning jobs to those who are already active members.

A minister might balk at the work involved in making these assignments. "It's easier to do it myself," he declares. He may be right, but the preacher who follows that practice will still be doing it himself ten years from now! He will also have robbed many people of the opportunity for development and service. He will not have been equipping the saints for the work of ministry.

Do not depend on volunteers alone for the available assignments. Some people will volunteer for anything (and everything!) while others will not function unless they are specifically asked. A word of encouragement to a shy but talented member can produce excellent results. Frequently the quieter members of your congregation will do better in a given job than some of the more forward members who might volunteer for it. A quiet Christian may feel that he has little or nothing to offer—simply because he does not know all of the different ways in which his service might be used in the church.

One job for each person—and no more than one job for each person—should be the goal. Such a goal will not be easily achieved, but it is worthwhile. The person who is overloaded will soon burn out, just like a fuse. When I came to a certain church, one man was the Bible-school superintendent, junior high youth sponsor, deacon, trustee, and bus driver. He did not need to be doing all of these jobs, but he was capable and he was willing. The jobs gravitated to him through his closeness to the previous preacher and his willingness to serve. In less than a year, he resigned from all of the duties, began attending church irregularly, and became a complainer. The change was at least partially caused by his previous overload.

Some respond to the suggestions offered in this chapter by saying, "But why spend all this time worrying about organization—giving people jobs—and the like? I just want to get out and do the Lord's work!"

This is the Lord's work! We can reach more people in less time through good planning and wise use of available manpower than by a hit-or-miss, catch-as-catch-can approach. The more members who are busy working for the Lord, the more work can be done. Doing things decently and in order is the Lord's way.

Organizational Requirements

Every church should have a constitution and bylaws. Such a document is normally required by the state to establish the church's legal existence as a nonprofit organization. The ownership of property will necessitate some legal procedures—at least the election of trustees. As a safeguard of the purposes and principles of the institution, protection is advisable. Each church is normally assigned a number that can be used in reporting for Social Security purposes or in identifying its tax-exempt status.

The congregation should seek competent legal counsel to make sure it meets the various government requirements. If the congregation has an attorney as a member, he will quite likely handle the procedures without charge. Other Christian attorneys in the area might also assist in this way. Even if the advice must be purchased, it is still a valuable investment.

As a minister, collect copies of constitutions and bylaws from sister congregations. These will be most helpful in designing such a document for the church with which you serve. Although each situation is different, the basics remain the same.

New Members

When someone becomes a member of the church, he should be made to feel at home, to sense his responsibility, and to begin training for service. Following are some of the specific steps that should be taken:

1. *Letter.* A few days after his baptism or transfer he should receive a letter from the minister, congratulating him on the decision and welcoming him to the church. The letter should contain a Christian Service Interest Sheet to be filled out. The minister can indicate that he (or an elder) will pick it up when he brings the new member packet to him within the next week.

2. *Packet.* A packet should be prepared for each new member. This should include such items as: baptismal certificate, church membership directory, bylaws, budget, and tracts (on the New Testament church, salvation, stewardship, etc.). Various Bible reading suggestions can be included, along with pertinent literature about different groups in the church, such as women's and youth programs. A packet of offering envelopes should be made available to the member with the other material. Some congregations give a copy of the New Testament to each new Christian (usually not to those who transfer membership).

The packet should be delivered personally by the minister and/or elder or deacon within two weeks of the day when the person was added to the church. When taking the material, the person should pick up the completed Christian Service Interest Sheet. Opportunity should be allowed for the person to ask questions. He should be enrolled for the next new member class.

3. *Class.* At least once each quarter a series of special lessons should be provided for every new member. These lessons

can be taught on Sunday mornings during the Bible-school period, on Sunday evenings before the worship hour, or at another time during the week. While the minister may lead in arrangements for the course, a competent elder or other church leader can teach much of the material. Some large churches have such a class running continuously.

My own practice has been to have four sessions on the following themes: the New Testament church (including a survey of church history); the Christian life (review how to become a Christian, changes involved, possible problems, principles to help solve them); my responsibility in the church (effectively led by an elder or deacon); my service (introducing various opportunities for work with the local assembly).

When first offered, all the sessions can be taught by the minister, but he should have several church leaders also attending the sessions in order to train them to teach future classes.

One week prior to the beginning of each course a personally typed letter should go to all new members who have been added since the last class, inviting them to attend. Naturally advance announcements will be made in the church paper and bulletin.

4. *Other Ways.* Some congregations have a "big brother" or "big sister" relationship. An older member is asked to be especially helpful to a specific new member. Various shepherding programs are available. Some congregations hold a quarterly reception for all new members. This serves as a kickoff to each new member class. The important result of all such programs is to involve every person actively and immediately into the total life of the church.

Attendance Record

The roll call card is the most effective tool for keeping accurate records of members' attendance. It is also an excellent source of prospect information. (Sample cards are shown in the Appendix.) Roll cards should be used at both morning and evening services. In smaller churches (or when starting such a program in a larger church) members need only fill out one card per day. In larger congregations, you will find advantages in having the cards filled in at each service. They may be placed in the pew racks, filled out during announcements, and passed to the aisles. Ushers should pick them up separately from the offering.

After the service, the minister should go through the cards. Separate the prospects so that they might receive a visitors' letter. Special needs should be followed up immediately. The remainder of the members' cards should be turned over to a secretary who keeps an attendance record.

The ideal person for such a job is an older member of the congregation—perhaps a former schoolteacher. Neatness, accuracy, and dependability are necessary for the job. The minister can check regularly to learn which members are not attending faithfully. This secretary can notify the minister and/or elders of any member who has missed a certain number of Sundays, and the person can then be contacted.

Such a record can also prove helpful when you consider prospective church leaders. If a man has been coming to church only once or twice a month, how could he possibly be ready to serve as a deacon? This can give a screening committee objective material on which to make a decision.

Christian Service Interest Sheets

As suggested earlier, these forms ought to be distributed to every new member. Present members can be encouraged to fill them out by a special emphasis. After announcing for two weeks that such a program is being instituted, the minister might preach on the use of one's talents at a morning worship service. These forms could be distributed at that time. Members would be asked to fill them in and leave them at the church. Additional copies could be handed out in Bible school and evening worship. Copies could be available on the next Sunday or two for those who have been absent.

When everyone has had an opportunity to complete and return a form, compare the list of those who responded with the membership roll. Mail a form with an urgent letter to those who have not yet completed one. Ask them to bring or mail the form to the church within the next two weeks. Remind them of it in the church paper. This should secure the participation of about seventy-five percent of the membership.

These forms can then be used to select committee members. Have a volunteer typist make one sheet for each category on the Christian Service Interest Sheet. On each sheet the typist then can list the names of all members who expressed interest in serving that way. The committee chairman attempting to locate nursery workers, for example, could find all of those who have already indicated a willingness to work in the nursery or launder clothing for it. He might also find a carpenter who could help repair a broken crib! If these records are kept up to date and used, they will help insure participation by many in the church program.

Recruiting Workers

Finding the name of someone who is interested in a specific job does not automatically fill a vacancy, however. The person may first need training. A brief inquiry into the individual's background and experience is helpful. In the case of a prospective teacher, you might let him serve as a guest teacher one Sunday and observe how he handles the class. Even one who has supposedly done a lot of teaching at another church may not be a good teacher.

Training sessions for present and future teachers may be arranged at times similar to those suggested for the new members class. If you are presently teaching, you will need to have an assistant ready to teach your class during the training period, if the training takes place during the Bible-school hour.

Another approach is suggested by Richard A. Myers. He has found that three-fourths of the present teachers are teaching because another teacher asked them. He suggests:

> In preparation for a teacher recruitment drive ask the present teachers to prepare a list of all of their students who are attending three out of four weeks. These represent persons who attend regularly if they are not sick or the family out of town. . . . After the family identification step has been completed, ask each teacher to call the families on the list. When the teacher calls, explain about the need for more teachers. Then ask if either the wife or husband or both, would be willing to help occasionally in the church school class which their child attends.[2]

Myers advises that the "helpers" then be used to take attendance, assist with discipline problems, and other minor duties at first. Those who work well (especially with young children) might be asked to teach some part of the lesson. After experience in this type of assistance, the individual may be introduced to the superintendent and suggested as a possible teacher. Whatever process one uses, the training of teachers must include on-the-job experience. This is a vital part of the individual's preparation.

Securing workers, like all interpersonal relationships, often requires delicate handling. The wise minister moves gradually and kindly—not forcing people into unwanted jobs nor failing to accept their actual limitations. At the same time, he will provide encouragement and challenge. He seeks to help equip the saints for the work of ministry.

Church Files

A good filing system helps the minister accomplish much of his work more smoothly. He knows that he can rapidly locate pertinent information at a moment's notice. The time he spends on research and study will be shortened. He will be able to accumulate a wealth of valuable material for his own use and the use of others.

In the local church, good records are crucial. The average congregation, however, has poor files—or no files. Following is a list of the information that should be kept on file at the church:

Members
1. New member cards (filled out by each person as he comes forward to be welcomed into the church family)
2. Christian Service Interest records (one sheet for each category)
3. Birthdays (listed by month and day; these may then be included in the church paper. The minister will be able to demonstrate his interest and concern if he will telephone personally each member on his/her birthday with a word of greeting)
4. Membership records (see below)
5. Attendance records (kept by a volunteer secretary on the basis of roll call cards)
6. Family folders (including counseling data and other information)

Ideally every church should have only one membership roll—an active membership roll. In reality, though, most congregations include some who came faithfully at one time, but are not attending regularly now. Until these people place their membership elsewhere or are removed from the records, they may be kept in an "inactive membership" file. The elders (or a membership committee that they appoint) should screen the total membership list at least once a year. Names may go from the active to inactive category or back depending on participation (attendance, giving, and service). If these names are kept on 3" x 5" cards, it will be simple to change them.

Each card should contain the name, address, telephone, and date of birth for the member. You could also include the date when that individual became a member of your church.

A book can be maintained (in addition to the card file) to provide a permanent record of all those who have come into the church. Many churches also find the publication of an annual membership directory, based on the active membership cards, to be helpful.

Non-Members
1. Visitors (Using one sheet for each letter of the alphabet, list visitors chronologically by date first attended.)
2. Prospects (When you choose to add a visitor to the prospect list, a card giving additional information can be prepared. Be sure to keep a duplicate card of any that have been given to callers.)

Church
1. Minutes of board meetings, elders' meetings, and congregational meetings
2. Business documents (orders, guarantees, insurance policies)
3. Legal documents (incorporation papers, bylaws, other official documents)
4. Publications (keep two copies of each weekly church paper and one copy of each Sunday bulletin; keep several samples of all other publications—reports, invitation leaflets, tracts, membership directories, invitation brochures, etc.)
5. Financial (records of income and expense should be preserved; the financial secretary may need to substantiate an amount given by a member for tax purposes)
6. History (clippings from the newspaper, important letters, and other items of interest for future generations)

Office Records
1. Tickler file (a folder for each month of the year and each day

of the current month in which reminders can be placed for things to be taken care of at specific times.)[3]
2. Correspondence (filed alphabetically by last name of the person being written; filed chronologically in the folder)
3. Programs/special events (men's banquet, vacation Bible school, music, dedication service, ordination, etc.)
4. Mission information (literature on missionaries supported by the church; Bible college catalogs)

Minister's Personal Records
1. Income (not only from the church but from speaking, writing, or other self-employment)
2. Mileage (business and medical mileage should be separately recorded for the most favorable tax benefits)
3. Sermons (card file by titles, with space to write the place and date when preached)
4. Baptisms
5. Weddings
6. Funerals
7. Personal correspondence (what you want to take with you upon leaving the church; material not specifically related to local church affairs)
8. Idea file (starter thoughts for sermons, articles, lessons)
9. Calls made
10. Business expenses

Each minister must maintain a filing system to include sermons, lessons, and articles he has prepared as well as the material for future ones. In filing, the simplest method is usually the best. Intricate sub-sub points on each topic, a tricky cross-reference system, and time-consuming entry processes all discourage one from keeping files up to date. Then what began as a filing system quickly becomes a piling system!

The sooner in life that one begins some filing system, the more helpful it can potentially become. While in college or seminary, the young minister should examine various methods being used by other ministers. From these and other plans about which he reads, he should develop a filing system suitable for his needs. Some suggestions on sermonic files are offered in Chapter 15. Other resources are listed at the end of this chapter. A well-developed filing system provides a wealth of help for the preparation of future messages.

Supplementary Reading

1. Dr. Richard A. Myers has a series of pamphlets on various aspects of church growth. Write for a list and current prices to: Richard A. Myers, 4821 Carvel Ave., Indianapolis, IN 46205.
2. Consider the following books as resources for new members: *Studies for New Converts* by Price Roberts; *Christian Growth* by Paul Benjamin; *Grounded Faith For Growing Christians* by Sam Stone; *Workbook on Christian Doctrine* by Joseph Dampier.
3. Helpful books:

A. Donald Bell, *How to Get Along With People in the Church*. Zondervan.

Lowell R. Ditzen, *The Minister's Desk Book*. Parker, 1968.

G. Stanley Joslin, *The Minister's Law Handbook*. Channel, 1962.

L. S. Richardson, *Handbook for the Church Office*.

W. S. Smith, *The Minister and His Study*. Moody, 1973.

Roy Sorenson, *How to Be a Board or Committee Member*. Association, 1953.

Related Projects

1. Compare the committee organization suggested in the text with that of your church. Collect sample committee lists (along with job descriptions) from other congregations. On the basis of these efforts, list ways in which your congregation's committee structure can be improved.
2. What short-term committee might become necessary in a typical church program? How should the nomination of new officers be conducted? How should long-range planning be handled?
3. Compare at least two of the following filing systems:
   a) Baker's Textual and Topical Filing System, published by Baker Book House.
   b) The Rossin-Dewey System, published by Donald F. Rossin Company, Inc., Minneapolis, MN 55415.
   c) The Memory-O-Matic System, published by the Mt. Vernon Foundation, 4205 37th St., Brentwood, MD 20722.

---

[1] Acts 14:23; 20:28
[2] Myers, *Recruiting Church School Teachers*, p. 41
[3] MacKenzie, *The Time Trap*, p. 162

Conclusion

After completing more than forty years in the pulpit, Olin Hay now teaches preaching at Atlanta Christian College. Asked to describe the rewards of the ministry, Dr. Hay responded, "I think of the soul-satisfying experience of standing up to preach convinced that I have a message from God. . . . Always a high moment for me is witnessing responses to the gospel message, hearing the good confession, and with one's own hands burying a believer in the water and into Christ. This has never become routine to me. I live in the glow of it for many days."

Turning to the fruits of a longer ministry, Olin Hay pictured the joy of seeing changed lives. He spoke of the challenge found in recruiting young "Timothys" for the preaching ministry. He concluded, "It is great to be a preacher. If I had my life to live over, I would not hesitate to do it again."

Nor would I.

May you have the same conviction!

The Christian ministry is not the easiest life, but nothing worthwhile comes cheap. Long hours, times of discouragement, temptations, times you feel like quitting—these will come. But they will also go. Beyond them, an enduring sense of fulfillment and satisfaction remains. People needed you, and you were there. People were lost, and now they are saved. You gave of yourself so that others might live. You learned to live close to God. Like Paul, you can say, "I thank Christ Jesus our Lord, who hath enabled me, for that he counted me faithful, putting me into the ministry" (1 Timothy 1:12, *King James Version*).

For these reasons, we press on. We would be faithful until death. We can sing with Howard A. Walter,

> I would be true, for there are those who trust me;
> I would be pure, for there are those who care;
> I would be strong, for there is much to suffer;
> I would be brave, for there is much to dare.
>
> I would be friend of all—the foe, the friendless;
> I would be giving, and forget the gift;
> I would be humble, for I know my weakness;
> I would look up, and laugh, and love, and lift.

APPENDIX

Section Outline

1. Questionnaire on the Minister's Work
2. Daily Plan Sheet
3. Minister's Contract
4. Board Meeting Agenda
5. Techniques of Visitation
     Calling Information Form
6. Sample Roll Call Cards
7. Wedding Checklist
8. Wedding Ceremony
9. Christian Service Interest Sheet

1. QUESTIONNAIRE ON THE MINISTER'S WORK (Ch. 2)

FACTS ABOUT YOURSELF   AGE GROUP
(Please check those that apply)
- ☐ Member of this church   under 18 ☐
- ☐ Member here more   18-21 ☐
  than ten years   21-31 ☐
- ☐ Elder, deacon, or trustee   31-51 ☐
- ☐ Teacher, youth sponsor,   51-65 ☐
  or class officer   over 65 ☐

(It is not necessary to sign your name)

I. YOUTH MINISTER'S WORK
I understand that the youth minister is to: (Check those that apply)
- ☐ a. teach a Bible-school class
- ☐ b. sponsor a youth group
- ☐ c. call on young people
- ☐ d. go to youth rallies
- ☐ e. direct VBS
- ☐ f. work in children's church
- ☐ g. call on sick and shut-ins
- ☐ h. maintain regular office hours
- ☐ i. assist in Sunday services
- ☐ j. preach once a month
- ☐ k. direct children's church
- ☐ l. call on adults
- ☐ m. plan outings for youth
- ☐ n. report regularly to senior minister
- ☐ o. work 2-2½ days a week
- ☐ p. work full time

II. VISITATION MINISTER'S WORK
I understand that the visitation minister is to: (Check those that apply)
- ☐ a. teach a Bible-school class

☐ b. call on sick and shut-ins
☐ c. maintain regular office hours
☐ d. work full time
☐ e. work 2-2½ days a week
☐ f. preach once a month
☐ g. call on inactive members
☐ h. call on prospective members
☐ i. assist in Sunday services
☐ j. report regularly to senior minister
☐ k. train other callers
☐ l. help plan church calling programs

III. SENIOR MINISTER'S WORK
What subjects would you like to hear discussed in his

sermons?_____

_____

What Scriptures discussed?_____

_____

Usually the minister's sermons are: (Check one)

☐ Extremely helpful   ☐ Some are helpful
☐ Often helpful   ☐ Most are not helpful

I think that our senior minister should spend, on the average, the following number of hours per week in each of these activities:

____ 1. Study for sermons and lessons
____ 2. Calling on prospective members
____ 3. Calling on absentees and inactive members
____ 4. Calling on the sick and shut-ins
____ 5. Calling on new members
____ 6. Attending committee and board meetings
____ 7. Attending class and church social gatherings
____ 8. Handling correspondence and other office work
____ 9. Counseling members who have problems
____10. Making telephone calls on church business

_____11. Conducting weddings and funerals
_____12. Counseling those who are to be married
_____13. Attending and/or leading church services
_____14. Participating in church activities outside of our congregation (area camp, campus ministry, or similar programs)
_____15. Participating in rallies or revivals at other area churches
_____16. Speaking for other churches, groups, and conventions (other than revivals)
_____17. Writing/editing the church paper, bulletins, and special reports
_____18. Meeting with staff members and assigning work
_____19. Running errands on church business (purchasing supplies, etc.)

I would like to see our minister spend more time in areas (answer by filling in numbers from the list above):

_____

For him to do this, I would be agreeable with his spending less time in areas (answer by number):

_____

IV. GENERAL EVALUATION
How do you feel the multiple ministry is working out here? (Check one)

☐ Very well   ☐ Well   ☐ Acceptably   ☐ Poorly

What suggestions do you have to improve the arrangement?

_____

_____

2. DAILY PLAN SHEET (Ch. 5)

AS I SEE TODAY	
*Priority	DATE _____

PEOPLE TO SEE   ADDRESS

_____ _____
_____ _____
_____ _____
_____ _____
_____ _____

Things to be done — OUT

_____ _____
_____ _____
_____ _____
_____ _____
_____ _____

Things to be done — CHURCH

_____ _____
_____ _____
_____ _____
_____ _____
_____ _____
_____ _____

LETTERS

_____ _____
_____ _____
_____ _____
_____ _____

PHONE CALLS   Person   Number

_____ _____
_____ _____
_____ _____

(Developed by John M. Byard, Bridgetown Church of Christ, Cincinnati, Ohio)

HOSPITAL	PATIENT	ROOM

Appointments and Meetings

Time		NOTES
6:00		
6:30		
7:00		
7:30		
8:00		
8:30		
9:00		
9:30		
10:00		
10:30		
11:00		
11:30		
12:00		
12:30		
1:00		
1:30		
2:00		
2:30		
3:00		
3:30		
4:00		
4:30		
5:00		
5:30		
6:00		
6:30		
7:00		
7:30		
8:00		
8:30		
9:00		
9:30		

3. MINISTER'S CONTRACT (Ch. 7)

(Developed by Arthur Merkle, Church of Christ, Wilmington, Ohio)

CONTRACTING PARTIES:
This working agreement shall be between _____

_____ as minister, and the _____

_____ as a corporate organization; and it shall be considered binding upon the congregation, its officers, their successors, and upon the minister.

EFFECTIVE DATE:
This agreement shall become effective on _____.

1. The provisions shall be agreed upon between the minister and the elders representing the congregation.
2. It shall be signed by the minister and the chairman of the board of elders.
3. It shall remain in effect until officially changed or canceled.

PROVISIONS FOR CHANGING OR CANCELING:
Changes shall be made in the provisions of this agreement by mutual consent, with the congregation being informed of any agreement made by the Elders.

1. Either party may cancel the contract with a written sixty (60) days notice given in the same spirit in which the contract was made.
2. Or with less than sixty (60) days, or more than sixty (60) days, by mutual consent.

THE CONGREGATION AGREES TO:
1. Accept such programs as advanced by the minister for promoting the work of the church, unless such program is deemed unscriptural by the elders, or too costly by a congregational vote.
2. Help organize the congregation under the eldership, help carry on a calling program that shall provide adequate over-

sight for every member of the church and prospect of the church, help provide work for every member of the flock, and help make the proper environment for worship at the stated meetings of the congregation.

3. Provide the following financial considerations for the minister:

   a. $_____ weekly salary

   b. $ _____ monthly house allowance (includes both housing and upkeep)

   c. $ _____ monthly utility allowance

   d. $_____ monthly automobile allowance

   e. $ _____ annual convention expense. This represents a minimum amount and more will be allowed by mutual consent.

   f. $ _____ quarterly checks are to be written to the minister in the amount spent by him for long distance calls in behalf of the church made on his phone.

   g. Progressive education clause: As a benefit to both the minister and the congregation, the church will pay admission fees and tuition fees for any educational courses the minister desires to take from schools, colleges, seminaries or correspondence courses, provided the courses are directly related to his services as a minister.

   h. The minister's salary shall be raised as the income of the congregation increases, as the cost of living index goes up, and as the merits of his work justify. An annual review of his salary will be made during the (month) elders meeting.

   i. A "petty cash" fund of $50 minimum advance is to be made available to cover expenses incurred in direct connection with church programming. An accurate record is to be kept of this fund and an annual audit submitted to the board at the January meeting.

   j. The church will pay the pension premiums of his retirement program.

   k. Workman's compensation and Blue Cross and Blue Shield will be carried on the minister and his family with the congregation paying the premiums.

4. Recognize the following as part of the agreement:
    a. The minister shall have a paid vacation at a convenient season of the year according to the following schedule:
        2 weeks and 2 Sundays after the first year
        3 weeks and 3 Sundays after five years
        4 weeks and 4 Sundays after ten years
    b. Attendance at conventions, retreats, camps, etc. are a part of the work of the minister.
    c. The minister is allowed to hold two weeks and two Sundays of revival meetings aside from commuting meetings each year. The elders are to personally fill the pulpit in his absence, or permit the use of missionary speakers or supply speakers at no cost to the minister.
    d. In case of illness on the part of the minister or his immediate family that would make it impossible for him to fill the pulpit or carry out the work of the church, the church will provide such leadership and speakers at no cost to the minister. Sick leave will be granted at the rate of 1¼ days per month or 15 days per year. Sick leave may accumulate but not to exceed 60 days without mutual agreement on the part of the contracting parties. The church board reserves the right to ask for a doctor's certificate as proof of sickness.
    e. The church agrees to recognize at least one day of complete rest each week for the minister.

THE MINISTER AGREES TO:
1. Personally fill the pulpit and lead the regular meetings of the church, except as provided above and except when speakers are permitted by the elders.
2. Labor in personal calling, study, preaching, teaching, office work, meetings, conferences, etc. (except as provided above) for a number of hours equal to the average working week of his elders.
3. Labor in excess of these hours an amount which shall equal or surpass that amount of time given by an elder with a regular job.
4. Present his programs to the elders for their ratification before submitting them to the congregation.
5. Preach the Word, as it is in the Book, in kindness and in love, and be governed by it in his walk of life.

BOTH PARTIES AGREE TO:
1. Regard the other with respect at all times (Romans 12:10).
2. Express confidence in the other publicly and often.
3. To give criticism personally and in a Christian manner.
4. Strive to follow the pattern of the New Testament church in all the organization, and the spirit of Christ in carrying out the plans.
5. Strive to teach the alien sinner and baptize him into Christ. Teach the members to "observe all things" whatsoever Jesus has taught.

SIGNED:

_____

Minister

_____

Chairman of the Elders

CONTRACT ADJUSTMENT SCHEDULE

Date Granted	Nature of Adjustment	Total Wage (if a salary adjustment)

4. BOARD MEETING AGENDA (Ch. 10)

(date of meeting)

I. Devotions

II. Roll Call

III. Acceptance of Minutes of (date of previous meeting)

IV. Treasurer's Report

V. Other Reports
  A. Elders
  B. Deacons
  C. Ministers
  D. Standing Committees
      1. Worship
      2. Christian Education
      3. Stewardship
      4. Evangelism and Nurture
      5. Property
      6. Fellowship and Service
  E. Long-Range Planning Committee
  F. Mission Committee (Recommendation attached)
  G. Church Bus
  H. Scout Program

VI. Any Other Business

VII. Adjournment and Closing Prayer

5. TECHNIQUES OF
VISITATION (Ch. 19)

I. WHAT TO TAKE
   A. Card with information about prospect
   B. Flashlight (for night calling)
   C. Tracts, church paper, other literature (available for you in the church office)
   D. Small Bible or New Testament (to be carried in pocket or purse)

II. WHAT TO DO
   A. When to call
      Afternoons and evenings are usually best; bad weather is a good time because most people stay home then.
   B. How to go
      It is preferable to go in pairs; one should be selected to be the leader inside and to do most of the talking (sit near the prospect, guide conversation); the silent partner takes care of children and pets.
   C. When not to enter the house
      Do not go in if the prospect is obviously busy or has company. Make an appointment for a return visit.
   D. Pray first
      Either silently or aloud before you leave the car. Ask God's help in your visit.
   E. Leave prospect card in the car
      Don't have anything in your hand as you go up to the door. Have the information in mind.

III. WHAT TO SAY
   A. Different types of calls
      Some calls will be primarily friendly, get-acquainted visits. You need not feel obligated to discuss the Scripture in detail unless the person shows definite interest and you feel able to teach him. If a question is raised that you cannot answer, admit that you don't know and offer to look up the answer and return and/or have one of the ministers stop by to explain. Teaching calls are best handled by appointment. Other calls may be made

without appointments, although having a definite time arranged with the family is certainly desirable.

B. General methods

1. *The Approach.* At the door, introduce yourself and mention that you are from the church. Ask, "May we stop in for a few minutes?" After a few minutes of friendly visiting, bring up the subject of church.

2. *The Appeal.* A good way to begin is to ask if they are members of a church somewhere. Find out which church they most recently attended. Let them know that we are happy to have them worship at our church.

If this is a get-acquainted call, you could give information about current activities, Bible classes for all members of the family, youth groups, etc.

In the case of a teaching call, you can begin by asking if they have noticed things different at our church compared to the other churches they have attended. Their questions can then be answered from Scripture. Never argue. Arguing only loses ground and does not convert anyone. Present the Scriptural truth and let the person make his decision.

In the case of those who need to transfer membership, at this time you can point out the values of having a church home in the community. Mention that we know their home church would encourage them to do this just as we encourage those who move from our area to locate with another congregation. Explain that they can transfer their membership without having first to send for a letter from the former church. If they are immersed believers in Christ they need only come forward during an invitation hymn and identify themselves.

3. *Decision.* Try to make some headway in each call. You might be guiding the person toward a decision to attend church Sunday, or perhaps to let you or the minister return to talk with him again. Those who seem ready should be encouraged to come forward and accept Christ. Explain what the minister will ask and what they will do (we are always prepared for baptism; no prior arrangements are necessary).

Leave with friendly concern. At times you might wish to have prayer with a family before you leave; at other times it will not seem appropriate.

IMPORTANT: Make notes of the visit, along with your name and the date, on the back of the "Calling Information Form" after you have driven a few blocks from the house. Return the card promptly to the church office or the minister.

CALLING INFORMATION FORM

Please call on _____ Phone _____

Address_____

Type of call: (write any other
                                                information below)
    Inactive member
    Shut-in
    Has visited regularly
    Attends regularly
    Has been called on before
    Good prospect
    Hasn't attended; name given by_____

Member of_____ Church

Other(s) in family are members here: _____

    Please write your name and the date visited on the opposite side, along with any other pertinent information. Return this form to the office as soon as possible. If the person is not home, leave literature and a note. Don't take this form with you to the door; fill it in later after leaving.

```
Westside
Church


              ROLL CALL

Name _____
Address _____
___ Visitor          ___ New Resident
___ Youth (under 18)
___ Not a Member Here
Where? _____
___ Considering Membership
___ Desire Minister to Call
___ Request Offering Envelopes
Invited By _____
Special Information _____
_____
```

6. SAMPLE ROLL CALL CARDS (Ch. 19)

The card at left is used to take attendance and receive information from the church attender. The card shown below is for new members, to be given to those who come forward at the invitation (see p. 181).

```
              WESTSIDE CHURCH

Name_____ Phone_____

Address_____

Have you been immersed? Yes___ No___ If not, do you wish to
be baptized now at the close of the service? Yes___ No___.

If not now, when would it be convenient? _____

_____


Formerly a member of _____

Address of church _____

Birthday (month and day only) _____
```

This card, printed on both sides, can be used either as an attendance card for church members or as an information card for visitors. This card is used at the Westwood-Cheviot Church of Christ in Cincinnati, Ohio.

MEMBER REGISTRATION (Visitors Please Use Other Side)

Date _____

☐ Worship I   ☐ Bible School   ☐ Worship II

Please use space below for messages to ministers — prayer requests — people in hospitals — change of address or phone — name and address of new residents.

Name _____
( )Mr. ( )Mrs. ( )Miss

_____

_____

_____

_____

_____

☐ Pastoral Call Desired   Phone _____

SILENT ROLL CALL

VISITOR REGISTRATION (Members Please Use Other Side)

Date _____

Name _____ Phone _____
( ) Mr. ( ) Mrs. ( ) Miss

Address _____ Zip _____

Member of _____ Church

☐ First Time Visitor   ☐ Attend here but not a member

☐ Send church paper   ☐ Interested in becoming a member here

☐ Request offering envelopes   ☐ Would like to learn more about the Bible

——— PLEASE CHECK PROPER GROUP ———

| Single | ☐ | Gr. 1-3 | ☐ | Jr. HI | ☐ | 18-24 | ☐ | 41-55 | ☐ |
| Married | ☐ | Gr. 4-6 | ☐ | Sr. HI | ☐ | 25-40 | ☐ | Over 55 | ☐ |

COMMENTS _____

_____

SILENT ROLL CALL

7. WEDDING
CHECKLIST (Ch. 20)

☐ Contact minister
(for both wedding
and rehearsal dates)
☐ Reserve the church
☐ Invitations ordered
☐ Contact organist
☐ Contact soloist

Contact florist:
☐ Candles
☐ Aisle runner cloth
☐ Kneeling bench
☐ Contact photographer
☐ Decide on rings
☐ Decide on wedding attire

Choose attendants:
☐ Best man
☐ Groomsmen
☐ Ring bearer
☐ Maid of honor
☐ Bridesmaids
☐ Flower girl
☐ Ushers
☐ Guest book

☐ Reception hostesses
☐ Gifts
☐ Clean up
☐ Motel reservations

Church building:
☐ Move communion table
☐ Move chairs
☐ Move pulpit
☐ Lights
☐ Reception arrangements
☐ Other
☐ Marriage license
☐ Appointment with minister
☐ Appointment with doctor

Type of ceremony desired:
☐ Repeat vows
☐ "I do"
☐ Single ring
☐ Double ring
☐ Private
☐ Open
☐ Formal dress
☐ Article to newspaper

8. WEDDING
CEREMONY (Ch. 20)

(Adapted by Edwin Hayden from P. H. Welshimer)

We are gathered together in the sight of God, and in the face of this company of friends, to join this man and this woman in the bonds of marriage; which is an honorable estate, established of God himself, who, when He made mankind, said, "It is not good for a man to be alone," and made a help-meet for him. This holy estate Christ adorned and beautified with His presence and first miracle that He wrought, at a wedding feast in Cana of Galilee. God has further honored it by choosing marriage as the symbol of the mystical union that is between Christ and His church—He is called the bridegroom and the church His bride. Marriage is, then, not to be entered into unadvisedly or lightly; but rather soberly, reverently, thoughtfully, discreetly, and in the fear of God. Into this holy estate these two come now to be joined. (If any man can show just cause why they may not lawfully be joined, let him now speak, or else hereafter forever hold his peace.)

Who gives this bride to be married?
(The Bride's father shall say, *I do*, or, *Her mother and I do.*)
Marriage is divine, and the home is one of God's most sacred institutions. It is established by the hand of God, and it is blessed and directed by His Word. Of the beginning we read that a man shall leave his father and mother and shall cleave unto his wife, so that they are no more two, but one flesh. The wise man of old said that "whoso findeth a wife, findeth a good thing," and of the virtuous woman that her price is far above rubies: "The law of kindness is on her tongue. She looketh well to the ways of her household, and eateth not the bread of idleness."

In the New Testament we are taught that the husband is to love his wife as Christ loved the church, and gave himself for it; also that the wife is to see that she reverence her husband.

Since you have come, therefore, each in your love of the other to present yourselves each to the other as the most precious and priceless gift that you could give, I shall ask you to take the following vows:

Do you, (Groom's name), promise to take this woman, (Bride's name), to be your lawful wedded wife, pledging before God, with these your friends as witnesses, that you will be to her a faithful, loving, and devoted husband; that you will provide for her and protect her; that you will honor her and love her; that you will remain with her in sickness and in health alike, in prosperity and adversity alike, and forsaking all others, will keep yourself to her and to her alone until death shall separate you?

(Answer: I do)

Do you (Bride's name), promise to take this man, (Groom's name), to be your lawful wedded husband, pledging before God, with these your friends as witnesses, that you will be to him a faithful, loving, and devoted wife; that you will honor him and love him; that you will remain with him in sickness and in health alike, in prosperity and adversity alike, and forsaking all others, will keep yourself to him and to him alone until death shall separate you?

(Answer: I do)

Do you wish to have these vows sealed with the gift of a ring?

(Answer: I do)

We have here, to be given by each to the other, the golden circlet which has been from time beyond measure the symbol of wedded love. The unending circle of the ring suggests the endlessness of real love. The purity of the precious metal suggests the purity of the married state as it is lived in accordance with the will and the laws of God. As often as you both shall see it, may it bring to memory the one glad moment when two lives become one. Take it, and place it on her hand.

(The Groom shall say, With this ring I thee wed.)

The like token will be given by the bride to the groom. As it shall surround his finger, may it betoken love and joy and peace surrounding and binding together both your lives. Take it, and place it on his hand with the same declaration.

You will join right hands to receive the solemn vows.

Now in accordance with the promises you have made and the vows you have taken, each to the other and in the presence

of an all-seeing God, and by the virtue of this authority vested
in me as a minister of the Gospel by the state of _____, I
declare you to be husband and wife, joined in the pure and holy
bonds of marriage. Let us remember then what Jesus our Lord
has said: "What God has joined together, let not man put asun-
der."

It is our wish and our prayer for you that love may never
go, but that it may rather grow, and make more rich and full
and blessed both your lives from this day forward.

A WEDDING PRAYER
By Helen Welshimer

God, give them length of days to live together
Upon this earth; and lend them grace, we pray.
To keep in dignity and peace and splendor
The bright new house that they have built today.
Oh, always may the new rooms be encircled
By walls of love, and may the faith two hold,
Each in the other, grow with time's long passing.
We do not pray that they shall garner gold
From years to be—for better to glean wisdom
Of Understanding, and to draw so near
Each to the other, that, though storms may threaten,
Their love will keep them guarded from all fear.
O teach them, God, on this, their bridal morning,
To walk life's path with fearless eyes, brave, gay;
To know that two who bear all things together
Will build a house that shall not pass away.

9. CHRISTIAN SERVICE INTEREST SHEET (Ch. 21)

Name _____ (check age group) Youth ☐ Adult ☐

Address_____ Phone_____

Place of Employment _____ Birthday_____

Please check the numbers below indicating the kinds of work in which you are talented or interested. Leadership training will be arranged for those desiring it.

CHRISTIAN EDUCATION
☐ 1. Bible-school teacher
☐ 2. Assistant teacher
☐ 3. Superintendent or ass't.
☐ 4. Youth fellowship sponsor
☐ 5. Vacation Bible school
☐ 6. Athletics
☐ 7. Records (secretary)
☐ 8. Librarian
☐ 9. Projectionist (show films and slides)

MUSIC
☐10. Song leading
☐11. Play piano
☐12. Play organ
☐13. Other instrument
☐14. Solo or group singing
☐15. Choir

PUBLIC RELATIONS
☐16. Call on prospects
☐17. Visit sick and shut-ins
☐18. Telephone
☐19. Correspondence
☐20. News, reporting
☐21. Ushering
☐22. Photography
☐23. Provide transportation

☐24. Hospitality to overnight guests
☐25. Campaign leader
☐26. Meals for evangelists
☐27. Greeter at the door

PERSONAL SKILLS
☐28. Bus driver
☐29. Art work, posters, etc.
☐30. Typing
☐31. Office work
☐32. Cut stencils
☐33. Cooking
☐34. Communion preparation
☐35. Carpentering
☐36. Painting
☐37. Floral arrangements
☐38. Plumbing
☐39. Electrical work
☐40. Care of grounds
☐41. Nursery work
☐42. Nursery laundry
☐43. Care of baptismal garments

DRAMATICS
☐44. Director or coach
☐45. Participant
☐46. Costumes, props, etc.

Bibliography

Adams, Jay E. *Shepherding God's Flock* (3 volumes; *The Pastoral Life, Pastoral Counseling*, and *Pastoral Leadership*). Grand Rapids, Michigan: Baker, 1975.

Anderson, Marvin. *Multiple Ministries—Staffing the Local Church*. Minneapolis: Augsburg Publishing, 1965.

Andrewes, Lancelot. *The Private Devotions of Lancelot Andrewes*. New York: Abingdon-Cokesbury, 1950.

Banker, John C. *Personal Finances for Ministers*. Philadelphia: Westminster, 1973.

Barber, Cyril J. *The Minister's Library*. Grand Rapids, Michigan: Baker, 1974.

Benjamin, Paul. *The Equipping Ministry*. Cincinnati: Standard Publishing, 1977.

Bounds, E. M. *Preacher and Prayer*. Grand Rapids, Michigan: Zondervan.

Bowman, George M. *How to Succeed With Your Money*. Chicago: Moody Press, 1974.

Brooks, Phillips. *Lectures on Preaching*. New York: E. P. Dutton & Co., 1877.

Carnegie, Dale. *How to Win Friends and Influence People*. New York: Simon & Schuster, 1937.

Christenson, Larry. *The Christian Family*. Minneapolis: Bethany Fellowship, 1970.

Coleman, Robert E. *The Master Plan of Evangelism*. Westwood, New Jersey: Revell, 1964.

Dayton, Edward and Ted Engstrom. *Strategy for Living*. Glendale, California: Regal Books, 1976.

Denton, Wallace. *The Role of the Minister's Wife*. Philadelphia: Westminster Press, 1962.

Engstrom, Theodore Wilhelm and R. Alec McKenzie. *Managing Your Time*. Grand Rapids, Michigan: Zondervan, 1972.

Gangel, Kenneth. *Competent to Lead*. Chicago: Moody Press, 1974.

_____. *So You Want to Be a Leader*. Harrisburg, Pennsylvania: Christian Publications, 1973.

Getz, Gene A. *The Measure of a Man*. Glendale, California: Regal Books, 1974.

Hendrix, Olan. *Management for the Christian Worker*. Libertyville, Illinois: Quill Publications, 1976.

Holck, Manfred, Jr. *Making It on a Pastor's Pay*. Nashville: Abingdon, 1974.

Hulme, William. *How to Start Counseling*. New York: Abingdon Press, 1955.

Johnson, H. Eugene. *Duly and Scripturally Qualified*. Cincinnati: Standard Publishing, 1975.

Joslin, G. Stanley. *The Minister's Law Handbook*. Manhasset, New York: Channel Press, 1962.

Jowett, J. H. *The Preacher: His Life and Work*. New York, Harper & Bros., 1912.

Kennedy, Gerald. *The Seven Worlds of the Minister*. New York: Harper & Row, 1968.

Kennedy, James D. *Evangelism Explosion*. Wheaton, Illinois: Tyndale, 1970.

Kent, Homer A., Sr. *The Pastor and His Work*. Chicago: Moody Press, 1963.

Kilinski, Kenneth, and Jerry Wofford. *Organization and Leadership in the Local Church*. Grand Rapids, Michigan: Zondervan, 1973.

Knott, Harold E. *How to Prepare a Sermon*. Cincinnati: Christian Restoration Association, 1977 (reprint).

_____. *How to Prepare an Expository Sermon*. Cincinnati: Christian Restoration Association, 1977 (reprint).

Koller, Charles W. *Expository Preaching Without Notes* (Vols. I & II). Grand Rapids, Michigan: Baker, 1962.

Kubler-Ross, Elisabeth. *On Death and Dying*. New York: Macmillan, 1969.

Lakein, Alan. *How to Get Control of Your Time and Your Life*. New York: P. H. Wyden, 1973.

Law, William. *A Serious Call to the Devout and Holy Life* (abridged edition). Philadelphia: Westminster, 1955.

Leas, Speed B. and Paul L. Kittlaus. *Church Fights: Managing Conflict in the Local Church*. Philadelphia: Westminster, 1973.

Leavitt, Guy P. *How to Be a Better Church Officer*. Cincinnati: Standard Publishing, 1962.

_____, revised by A. Leon Langston. *Superintend With Success*. Cincinnati: Standard Publishing, 1980.

Lewis, C. S. *The Screwtape Letters*. New York: Macmillan, 1942.

Lightfoot, J. B. *St. Paul's Epistle to the Philippians* (reprint). Grand Rapids, Michigan: Zondervan, 1953.

Lloyd-Jones, D. Martyn. *Preaching and Preachers*. Grand Rapids, Michigan: Zondervan, 1972.

Lowder, Paul D. *Let Us Pray—A Minister's Prayer Book*. Nashville: The Upper Room, 1963.

Mace, David R. *Success in Marriage*. New York: Abingdon, 1958.

MacKenzie, R. Alec. *The Time Trap*. New York: AMACOM, 1972.

McBurney, Louis. *Every Pastor Needs a Pastor*. Waco, Texas: Word, 1977.

McCabe, Joseph E. *How to Find Time for Better Preaching and Better Pastoring*. Philadelphia: Westminster, 1973.

McGarvey, J. W. "Church Government," *The Missouri Christian Lectures*. St. Louis: Christian Publishing Co., 1892.

Murch, James D. *Christian Education in the Local Church*. Cincinnati: Standard Publishing, 1943.

_____. *The Christian Minister's Manual*. Cincinnati: Standard Publishing, 1965.

Nordland, Francis. *The Unprivate Life of a Pastor's Wife*. Chicago: Moody Press, 1972.

Oates, Wayne E. *The Christian Pastor*. Philadelphia: Westminster, 1951.

_____. *Confessions of a Workaholic*. New York: World Publishing Co., 1971.

Pentecost, Dorothy H. *The Pastor's Wife and the Church*. Chicago: Moody Press, 1964.

Perry, C. M. *Pastoral Problems and Procedures*. Grand Rapids, Michigan: Baker, 1974.

Perry, Lloyd. *A Manual for Biblical Preaching*. Grand Rapids, Michigan: Baker, 1965.

Rassieur, Charles L. *The Problem Clergymen Don't Talk About*. Philadelphia: Westminster, 1976.

Richards, Lawrence O. *Creative Bible Teaching*. Chicago: Moody Press, 1971.

_____. *A New Face for the Church*. Grand Rapids, Michigan: Zondervan, 1970.

_____. *A Theology of Christian Education*. Grand Rapids, Michigan: Zondervan, 1976.

Robertson, A. T. *The Glory of the Ministry*. Grand Rapids, Michigan: Baker (reprint), 1967.

Robinson, William. *The Administration of the Lord's Supper*. Birmingham, England: Berean Press, 1959.

Scherzer, Carl J. *Ministering to the Physically Sick*. Englewood Heights, New Jersey: Prentice-Hall, 1963.

Schuller, Robert. *Your Church Has Real Possibilities*. Glendale, California: Regal Books, 1974.

Shedd, Charlie. *Time for All Things*. Nashville: Abingdon, 1962.

Simpson, F. Dale. *Leading the First Century Church in the Space Age*. Abilene, Texas: Quality Printing, 1972.

Smith, Wilbur. *The Minister in His Study*. Chicago: Moody Press, 1973.

Southard, Samuel. *Pastoral Authority and Personal Relationships*. Nashville: Abingdon, 1969.

Standard Manual for Funeral Occasions. Cincinnati: Standard Publishing, 1953.

Stewart, James S. *Heralds of God*. London: Hodder and Stoughton, 1952.

Stott, John R. W. *The Preacher's Portrait.* Grand Rapids, Michigan: Eerdmans, 1961.

Sugden, Howard and Warren Wiersbe. *When Pastors Wonder How.* Chicago: Moody Press, 1973.

Trueblood, Elton. *The Company of the Committed.* New York: Harper & Bros., 1961.

————. *The Yoke of Christ.* New York: Harper & Bros., 1958.

Turnbull, Ralph G. *A Minister's Obstacles.* Westwood, New Jersey: Revell, 1964.

Wagner, C. Peter. *Your Church Can Grow.* Glendale, California: Regal Books, 1976.

Weed, Michael R. (editor) *The Minister and His Work.* Austin, Texas: Sweet, 1970.

Whitesell, Faris D. *The Art of Biblical Preaching.* Grand Rapids: Zondervan, 1950.

Wynn, J. C. *Pastoral Ministry to Families.* Philadelphia: Westminster, 1957.

Index

243

Scripture Index